PRACTICAL GREEN REMODELING

Down-to-Earth Solutions for Everyday Homes

BARRY KATZ

The Taunton Press

The Taunton Press
Inspiration for hands-on living®

The Taunton Press, Inc., 63 South Main Street, PO Box 5506, Newtown, CT 06470-5506

e-mail: tp@taunton.com

Editor: Peter Chapman

Copy editor: Diane Sinitsky

Indexer: Jay Kreider

Cover design: Renato Stanisic

Interior design: Chika Azuma

Layout: Chika Azuma

Illustrator: Melanie Powell

Cover photographer: Front cover: Greg Hursley; Back cover: (clockwise from left) Charles Bickford, courtesy *Fine Homebuilding* magazine, © The Taunton Press, Inc. (2), Jack Thompson, Bradley Khouri

The following names/manufacturers appearing in *Practical Green Remodeling* are trademarks: AdvanTech®; AirTap™; American Olean™; Bark House®; Bio-Glass™; CaesarStone®; Cradle to Cradle; Dumpster®; Eco-Terr®; Energy Star®; Flor™; Google™; Green Seal®; HardiePanel®; Heat Mirror®; Highland Craftsmen Inc.®; The Home Depot®; IceStone®; IKEA®; InterfaceFLOR™; Kill A Watt™; Lego®; LiveRoof®; Marmoleum®; Marvin Integrity®; Metlund®; Modern Bamboo™; Osmo Polyx®; PaperStone™; Polaris®; Raydoor®; Richlite®; Safecoat®; Sawfish™; SkyBlend™; SmartWood™; Spaceloft® Insul-Cap™; Styrofoam™; Trex®; Viesso®; Warmboard®; Whitfield®; YOLO Colorhouse®.

© **Mixed Sources**

Product group from well-managed forests, controlled sources and recycled wood or fiber

FSC www.fsc.org Cert no. SCS-COC-000648
© 1996 Forest Stewardship Council

Library of Congress Cataloging-in-Publication Data

Katz, Barry.

Practical green remodeling : down-to-earth solutions for everyday homes / author, Barry Katz.

   p. cm.

Includes index.

ISBN 978-1-60085-088-2

1. Dwellings--Remodeling. 2. Sustainable construction. I. Title.

TH4816.K38 2010

643'.7--dc22

2010028593

Printed in the United States of America

10 9 8 7 6 5 4 3 2 1

DEDICATION

For Adam and Sophie

ACKNOWLEDGMENTS

Many people helped make this book possible—too many to list them all. But I would be remiss if I failed to thank the following people individually.

For starters, this book would not exist if Steve Culpepper had not encouraged me to write it in the first place. Thank you, Steve.

To the many homeowners who graciously allowed their newly green homes to be included and to all of the architects, designers, and contractors who answered an avalanche of questions and provided reams of information, I am deeply grateful. Special thanks to Michael and Cindy Klement for their warm hospitality during my visit to Ann Arbor.

I am indebted to Scott Miller and Ed Friedland for their advice on contracts and the business of publishing; Alan Simmons for sharing data on sales of green homes; Ryan Milligan for research and fact checking; Laurel Boudreau for some last-minute advice about green cleaning products; and Brandon Tinianov at Serious Materials for sharing a wealth of knowledge about high-performance windows.

Two friends were especially generous with their time. Constantine Valhouli carved out a substantial block of his for a careful reading of the manuscript and made many invaluable suggestions. Much of what I know about water issues, local as well as global, I learned from Wylie Sawyer.

Many thanks to all of the talented and dedicated staff at The Taunton Press; to Diane Sinitsky for her meticulous copy editing; and most especially to Peter Chapman, my astonishingly patient editor, who with unfailing good humor deftly guided a first-time author through the long process of writing this book. It would not be what it is without him.

Finally, my undying love and gratitude go to my son, Adam, whose energy and enthusiasm helped me keep the momentum going, and to my daughter, Sophie, who gently, but persistently, pointed out the importance of actually finishing the book.

✳ INTRODUCTION

First things first: This is not a how-to book. Unlike a lot of books about home remodeling, there are no step-by-step instructions, no tool or materials lists, no advice from the pros for the do-it-yourselfer. Instead, this is a what-to book. After all, before you get to the how-to stage, you need a vision of what you want to do. In this book, I suggest some new ways of thinking about what makes for a successful remodeling project. Is it enough to create more living or storage space, a more convenient floor plan, a nicer kitchen or bathroom? Is it enough simply to make your home more attractive?

BEFORE

Here's another question. What creates value? One of the first things homeowners want to know about any improvement is, will it be a good investment? Will the added value justify the expense? But what is our standard for judging value? Is it just about how much the home will sell for?

Most home improvements do not add as much value to the house as they initially cost. A new kitchen that costs $50,000 typically adds less than $40,000 to the home's resale value. On average, most renovations add anywhere from 65% to 85% of their cost to the home's value. So why do we do it? The answer for most people is that part of the value comes from the added enjoyment or functionality they get from the newly improved home. You might, for example, select a particularly attractive ceramic tile for your bathroom just because you like it, even though it costs more than a cheaper option that doesn't turn you on. When you eventually sell the house, it is unlikely that your choice of tile will alter the price a buyer is willing to pay. But every day, when you walked into the bathroom it gave you pleasure. That's worth something.

Adding a deck to the back of your house typically adds about 75% of its cost to the home's value. But over the years you'll spend many summer evenings relaxing on that deck, barbecuing, entertaining friends and family. The pleasure you get from having that deck means that, for you, it was money well spent.

But what about less tangible—or at least, less visible—improvements? If you choose non-toxic materials that don't endanger your family's health, isn't that worth something, even if the materials cost slightly more? What is the return on an investment that provides improved indoor air quality, reducing the likelihood that your children will suffer with allergies or asthma?

What if you have strong convictions about the environment? You might happily donate money to the World Wildlife Fund to help them fight deforestation in tropical rain forests. You don't expect any return other than the knowledge that you helped a little bit. But you know that if enough people do the same, it will have a meaningful impact.

But what about spending a little more for sustainably harvested lumber? It won't have any direct impact on your daily life. But as more people make that choice, it grows the market for sustainable lumber, which drives down the price. As the price goes down, illegal harvesting in rain forests becomes less profitable and a vital resource is preserved. Whether any particular choice adds to your enjoyment of the house, or your sense of pride in being a good citizen of Planet Earth, it is clear that not every decision you make is based on its value as an investment.

Still, in many ways, green remodeling is a sound financial investment. Investing in energy efficiency might cost a bit more up front, but you come out way ahead because the savings on your utility bills are greater than the small increase in your mortgage payment. It is an investment that pays for itself and then continues paying dividends as long as you own your home—and when you go to sell it. A growing body of evidence suggests that buyers are willing to pay more for energy-efficient green homes and that such homes sell faster than nongreen homes. As more people become aware of the benefits of living in healthy, energy-efficient homes, it is very likely those homes will sell at a significant premium, while energy hogs with poor indoor air quality will lose value.

By presenting a selection of successful green remodeling projects, in all price ranges from all over the country, I hope to inspire you to think about what you might do to make your own home greener. I also hope to give you a wish list and a what-to list: what to ask your architect or designer; what to ask your contractor; what to ask the heating contractor; what to ask a landscape designer; what to ask about the materials that will go into your remodel; what to ask about indoor air quality; what to think about when choosing lighting, appliances, plumbing fixtures, cabinets, countertops, paint, flooring . . . in short, what to look for in the way of greener, more sustainable everything.

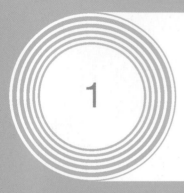

1 WHY GO GREEN?

What would it be like to live in a house that made us feel good? Not just by virtue of its fine proportions and attractive design, but a house that could actually make us healthier. And not only that, but a house that didn't waste energy, squander scarce resources, or harm the environment. And, just for good measure, a house that was economical to operate, required little maintenance, and was more valuable than its neighbors. In other words, what would it be like to live in a green home?

All across the country, there has been a dramatic increase in the number of homeowners who want to know the answer to that question. Why are so many people suddenly interested in making their homes greener?

AFTER

Win, win, win, win: Whether your remodeling plans call for a few modest improvements or a dramatic whole-house makeover, doing it green can make your home more environmentally friendly, healthier to live in, and more economical to maintain and operate.

BEFORE

WHY GREEN, WHY NOW?

Perhaps the green movement is because people are finally waking up to the realization that our planet is in serious trouble. More and more, we can't help wondering what kind of world we are passing on to our children and grandchildren and what kind of problems we are saddling them with. Every day we see news accounts of rising global temperatures, melting glaciers, changing weather patterns that are starting to affect food production, serious water shortages, and the depletion of wildlife habitat, biodiversity, and natural resources proceeding at an alarming rate. And more and more, we are starting to ask ourselves what we can do about it.

The scope of the problem seems so vast that we often wonder how anything we do as individuals can possibly make a difference. Yet single-family homes in the United States produce 21% of atmospheric carbon dioxide emissions, the most prevalent greenhouse gas responsible for global warming. Our homes, at least, are something we, as individuals, do have the power to change. Remodeling a home in ways that make it greener offers an excellent opportunity to stop being part of the problem and to become part of the solution (see the sidebar below).

green view

Most experts agree that improving the energy efficiency of buildings is one of the most cost-effective and readily achievable paths to large-scale reductions in greenhouse gas emissions. Consider this: If just one-quarter of the single-family homes in the United States reduced their energy use by 20%, it would prevent 48 million tons of CO_2 from being released into the atmosphere each year. That's the equivalent of removing nearly 10 million cars from the road. Small streams feed mighty rivers.

Small gaps around windows and doors, plumbing pipes, and electrical penetrations allow large amounts of heat to escape. Sealing those gaps is quick, easy, and inexpensive—and can make a big difference in your home's energy efficiency and comfort.

REMODELING IS INHERENTLY GREEN

In many ways, the very act of remodeling is inherently green. Here's why. You are upgrading a house that already exists rather than building a new one, with all the attendant strain on natural resources that involves. So you are keeping significant amounts of material—lumber, hardwood flooring, copper tubing, cabinets—and continuing to use those resources rather than sending them to a landfill and replacing them with virgin material. And you are continuing to live in a place where infrastructure—roads, sewers, utility lines—is already in place, rather than moving to a new sub-division where previously undeveloped land needs to be cleared, dug up, and paved over and where new water and sewer lines and electric, telephone, and TV cables must be installed, all at great cost both financially and in the consumption of resources.

Excessive energy consumption, and the negative environmental impacts associated with producing all that energy, can be dramatically reduced (and so can your utility bills). Choices as simple and inexpensive as plugging air leaks or switching to more efficient lightbulbs can have an enormous impact. And that's just the beginning.

Reducing a home's energy consumption by 25% to 40% or even more is not uncommon in green remodeling projects and is well within reach for most people. And today, the holy grail of a net-zero energy home—that is, one that produces as much energy as it consumes by employing renewable energy systems like solar panels—is no longer just a dream but, for an increasing number of homeowners, a reality.

But there is more to green remodeling than just improving energy efficiency. Greener homes not only consume less fossil fuel, but they also make more efficient use of all kinds of natural resources. They reduce waste, making innovative use of materials with recycled content; extending the useful life of valuable materials that once would have ended up in a landfill; using lumber and other materials more efficiently; and conserving water and energy.

Going green also means making homes healthier. Americans spend, on average, 90% of their time indoors. For young children and senior citizens, the percentage is higher. But the air indoors is commonly two to five times as polluted as outdoor air and much more than that in some homes. It is no coincidence that rates of asthma and allergies in the United States have skyrocketed in recent years.

Indoor pollutants are blamed for a vast array of symptoms including headaches, fatigue, dizziness, sore throats, eye irritation, nasal congestion, and rashes. Exposure to toxins such as formaldehyde and volatile organic compounds (VOCs) is one of the prime culprits. These compounds are found in many building materials, such as plywood, particleboard, adhesives, paints and finishes, and even fabrics, carpeting, and wall coverings. But there are alternatives if you know where to look.

In many homes, excessive moisture fosters the growth of mold and mildew, posing serious health risks. And even the cleaning products used every day in millions of homes can have negative impacts on our health. We can do better.

Finite resources

Unavoidably, the very act of building and remodeling homes uses up a lot of stuff. People have to live somewhere, and the population is growing rapidly. So we're using a lot more of everything that goes into houses, from lumber to steel to a wide range of building products derived from petroleum and natural gas, such as paints, plastics, and roofing. But is there an infinite supply of these things? Obviously, there is not.

If the earth contains a finite amount of natural resources, which clearly it must, and each year we keep using up those resources faster than we did the year before to meet the housing needs of a growing population, which we certainly are doing, that is obviously not something that can be sustained indefinitely or, indeed, for very much longer.

It took 125 years to extract the first trillion barrels of oil from the earth; it will take 30 years to extract the next trillion. That's not sustainable financially *or* environmentally. So we are simply going to have to find ways to use less energy and to produce clean, renewable energy. And we will need to find ways to use less of things that cannot be easily replaced or regenerated. And we will need to find ways to extend the useful life of materials that are already in use.

All it takes to turn this mess around is for us to start making some informed choices. But what are those choices? And why do so many people fail to seize the opportunity? Largely, it's because we are only just beginning to understand the importance of going green: to the environment, to the economy, and to our own families. There is also the widely held misperception that going green is inherently more expensive.

WORKING WITH GREEN BUILDERS AND ARCHITECTS

While an increasing number of architects, designers, and builders have started offering sustainable options to their clients, the vast majority aren't there yet. Most of the time, homeowners planning a remodel are simply unaware of what effects their choices will have. But imagine what it would be like if professionals in the industry were required to disclose the true environmental impact of the choices made by their clients.

Let's say you've decided to remodel your house. Perhaps you'd like to redo the kitchen—make it more spacious and more convenient for cooking and socializing. Maybe you'd like to add a family room where you can relax, hang out with your kids, play games, or watch a little TV. Maybe your

WHAT IS A NET-ZERO ENERGY HOME?

A net-zero energy home is one that produces as much energy as it consumes over the course of a year. To achieve net-zero or near-zero energy use, the first step is to wring every drop of inefficiency possible out of the house. Using techniques such as air sealing; high-performance insulation and windows; passive solar features; efficient lighting, appliances, and mechanical systems; and keeping the square footage down with efficient space planning, the amount of energy a home consumes can be greatly reduced.

When a home's energy demands are sharply reduced, it becomes feasible to supply those needs with on-site renewable energy from sources such as photovoltaic (PV) solar panels, solar hot-water heating, and in some locations wind or small-scale hydropower.

This zero energy remodeling project in Califon, New Jersey, was performed by Asdal Builders in conjunction with the NAHB Research Center.

Even a simple kitchen remodel provides lots of options for going green, like brightening up the space with more daylight, using nontoxic materials and finishes, and installing energy-efficient appliances.

family is growing and you need an extra bedroom or two, or you want a cozy new master suite to serve as a refuge when those adorable toddlers turn into noisy teenagers. Maybe you'd simply like to make your home more attractive. You want to freshen it up with new siding, paint, wallpaper, or flooring. Or update a bathroom or two with new tile, cabinets, and fixtures. Maybe you'd like the house to be brighter, with more sunshine and better lighting. Or you might simply want to be more comfortable—fewer drafts, warmer in the winter, and cooler in the summer.

Now let's say you have made some basic decisions about what you want to do and are ready to meet with a contractor to discuss how to do it. Typically, you will be asked a series of questions about your needs and preferences for every part of the house: how much space you need, what you want it to look like, and, of course, how much you are willing to spend. But you should ask some questions, too.

If you want to make your home healthier, more valuable, more economical to operate and maintain, and less of a strain on the planet's resources—in short, greener—asking questions and knowing what questions to ask is half the battle. Fortunately, one question you don't have to ask is whether you care more about improving your home and protecting your family or improving your carbon footprint and protecting the environment. Self-interest or global interest? It doesn't much matter because they both get you to the same place. Greener homes are better for your pocketbook and your family's health, as well as for the economy and the planet's health.

This book will arm you with many questions and, I hope, a few answers, too. So when you are ready to start your next remodeling project, be it large or small, don't be afraid to ask questions—lots of them. And just keep asking until you get the right answers.

HIRING A GREEN CONTRACTOR: WHAT TO ASK BEFORE YOU SIGN

Depending on where you live, you may or may not be able to find a contractor who has a great deal of experience with green remodeling. If there are no experienced green remodelers in your area, look for someone who takes pride in doing quality work, is open to learning about new and better methods and materials, and is eager to help you achieve your goals for a greener home. Then you and/or your architect will need to provide clear instructions for all of the sustainable strategies you want to incorporate.

If you do find a contractor who professes to have green remodeling expertise, here are some questions to ask:

※ How many green remodels have you completed?

※ Do you have any green training or certifications?

※ What do you think are the three most important energy-efficiency measures I should consider for my project?

※ What type of insulation do you prefer and how much do you recommend?

※ What kind of HVAC system do you think is most appropriate for my house?

※ What steps do you take to reduce job-site waste?

※ Are there materials from the remodeled portions of my house that can be reused?

※ How do you deal with improving indoor air quality?

※ Can you show me a few of your completed jobs and explain what makes them green?

And, as always, get a list of references and call two or three of them. Ask how satisfied they were with the contractor in general and how the house is performing, especially with regard to comfort and energy efficiency.

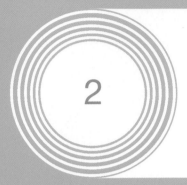

THE THREE FUNDAMENTALS OF GREEN REMODELING

2

There are literally hundreds of sustainable strategies that can be employed in green remodeling—from improving insulation to using materials with recycled content and avoiding materials that off-gas toxic fumes—but, to my mind, they all fall into three main categories. I refer to these broad classifications as the three fundamentals of green remodeling: energy efficiency, resource conservation, and healthy living environments.

Waste not. This unique bathroom shelf, one of several items hand-crafted from locally sourced fallen wood for a green condo remodel in Washington, D.C. (see p. 146), adds character and warmth without consuming virgin materials.

Energy efficiency is pretty straightforward. It is estimated that homes in the United States are responsible for 21% of global warming, which is caused primarily by the burning of fossil fuels. Substantial reductions are not only possible but also surprisingly cost-effective and easy to achieve. Typically, the homeowner's energy-cost savings will pay for the cost of energy upgrades in a short time—anywhere from a few months to a few years. Switching to energy-saving light-bulbs, adding a programmable digital thermostat, and installing low-flow showerheads all have a payback of less than a year. A new geothermal heat pump system's payback might take four to six years, depending on what kind of system it's replacing and on the cost of energy where you live. The payback on photovoltaic solar panels is likely to be more than 10 years unless you live in a state with a generous incentive program. Leveraging these costs by rolling them into an amortizing mortgage can improve the financial advantage considerably.

Improving your home's energy efficiency will save you money, but for many homeowners, the environmental benefits of energy efficiency are just as important. There are more than 75 million single-family homes in the United States. If even a small percentage of those could achieve, say, a 25% reduction in energy use, that would make a big dent in our fossil fuel consumption and its contribution to the climate crisis.

Resource conservation covers a lot of territory. The building and remodeling industry is a voracious consumer of a wide array of natural resources, many of which are already becoming scarce. We are using up a lot of things that we cannot afford to run low on. Water shortages are becoming acute in many areas, causing untold problems for industry, farmers, and homeowners. Deforestation is responsible for a vast increase in atmospheric CO_2, as well as soil erosion, habitat loss, and a loss of biodiversity at rates not seen since the last great extinction 65 million years ago.

More than ever before, we need to make our homes more resource efficient. We need to find ways to use less lumber, less water, less steel, fewer virgin materials of all kinds: in short, less of everything. But, as we'll see, that doesn't have to mean sacrificing our homes' beauty or comfort. It just means being smarter about what materials we use and how we use them.

Healthy living environments are shaped by several factors. Many commonly used building materials contain harmful chemical compounds that off-gas into the air we breathe.

Programmable thermostats save energy by automatically turning the temperature down while you're sleeping or at work and turning it up again at predetermined times. Most models can store different schedules for each day of the week. The energy savings can pay back the cost of the thermostat in six to eight months.

WHAT MAKES A REMODEL GREEN?

Every green remodel is different, and each one requires individual solutions to its unique challenges and opportunities. But they all have three things in common: energy efficiency, resource conservation, and healthy living environments. Let's take a quick look at a few of the features that fall into each category.

Energy Efficiency
- A tight, well-insulated building envelope
- Efficient lighting and appliances
- Efficient water heating and space heating and cooling
- Passive solar heating
- Natural ventilation
- Ample daylight

Resource Conservation
- Efficient use of construction materials to minimize waste
- Materials with recycled content
- Reclaimed materials
- Rapidly renewable materials
- Water-saving plumbing fixtures

Healthy Living Environments
- Formaldehyde-free plywood and particleboard
- Low-VOC or zero-VOC paints and finishes
- Properly vented combustion heating equipment
- Kitchen range hoods vented to the outside
- Humidity control

There are a great many things you can do in each category to make your remodeling project greener. But how many of them do you need to be able to call your remodeled home green?

You don't have to do everything. Some things won't be applicable to your particular project, and some may not make sense to do for other reasons. But the bottom line is this: To call a remodel green, it needs to address each of the three fundamentals in some way. If it's not energy efficient, it's not green. If it doesn't conserve materials or water or reduce the strain your home places on the environment, it's not green. And if it's not healthy to live in, it's not green.

The warm glow of the built-in cabinets and wood flooring shown here was brought out using tung oil, a durable, natural, low-VOC alternative to petroleum-based polyurethane.

So choice of materials is critical for healthy indoor air quality. But so are moisture management, adequate ventilation, and proper air filtration. Even your choice of furnishings and cleaning supplies will impact your total indoor environmental quality. For everyone concerned with their health (isn't that just about everybody?), and especially for families with young children, a home with healthy indoor environmental quality is one of the prime benefits of green remodeling.

CROSSOVER STRATEGIES

Not all green strategies fit neatly into one category. In most cases, a particular green strategy will satisfy more than one of the three fundamentals. For example, construction details designed to prevent unwanted moisture will not only foster a healthy living environment by inhibiting mold and dust mites, which thrive in high humidity, but also make the house more durable, which helps conserve both resources and energy because the house will require fewer repairs and less maintenance.

Using reclaimed materials or products with recycled content obviously conserves natural resources such as timber, but it also conserves energy. Every product or material represents a certain amount of *embodied energy*—that means the sum total of all the energy that is expended in harvesting or extracting the raw materials from the earth, shaping those raw materials into the things we use (everything from 2x4s to washing machines), transporting them to the point of use (your house), and eventually hauling them off to the landfill or incinerator at the end of their useful lives. Giving materials a new lease on life greatly reduces the amount of embodied energy associated with building and remodeling homes.

Conserving water, an increasingly urgent need in our H_2O-constrained world, also reduces energy consumption. Low-flow faucets and showerheads and efficient appliances consume less water, which means that less water needs to be heated, whether by oil, gas, or electricity. Water heating typically consumes 18% to 20% of a home's total energy use. And just getting the water to your house in the first place uses a lot of energy; whether you have a private well or are connected to a municipal water system, both require pumps that burn electricity. In California, for example, 25% of the state's electricity is consumed by moving water from one place to another.

This chapter will provide a broad overview of the methods and materials that fall under each of the three fundamentals. Later chapters will provide more detail on each of the green strategies outlined below.

FUNDAMENTAL 1: ENERGY EFFICIENCY

The one question I'm asked more than any other about green remodeling is, "How much more will it cost?" (For some reason, most people automatically assume that it costs more to go green.) But there really isn't a good answer to this question because, quite simply, it is the wrong question. When you look at the economics of investing in energy efficiency, it becomes abundantly clear that the right question to ask is how much more would it cost *not* to go green!

Improving your home's energy efficiency is one of the best investments you will ever make. Unlike the stock market, where any securities you buy might either make money or lose money, there is no chance that your investment in energy efficiency will turn bearish on you. Energy-efficient lightbulbs will not suddenly change course and start using more energy than standard incandescent bulbs. In fact, most energy improvements will not only pay for themselves but also will continue to pay dividends in terms of lower utility bills as long as you own your home.

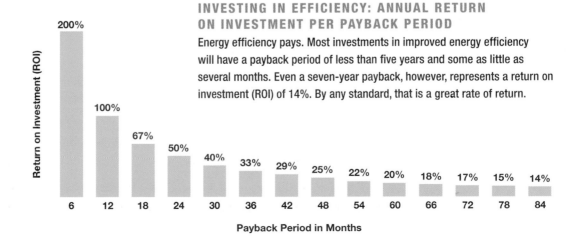

INVESTING IN EFFICIENCY: ANNUAL RETURN ON INVESTMENT PER PAYBACK PERIOD

Energy efficiency pays. Most investments in improved energy efficiency will have a payback period of less than five years and some as little as several months. Even a seven-year payback, however, represents a return on investment (ROI) of 14%. By any standard, that is a great rate of return.

Return on Investment (ROI)

6	12	18	24	30	36	42	48	54	60	66	72	78	84
200%	100%	67%	50%	40%	33%	29%	25%	22%	20%	18%	17%	15%	14%

Payback Period in Months

WHAT IS A GREEN HOME WORTH?

Are green homes really worth more? Although green homes are still a relatively new trend in the real estate market, evidence is starting to mount that they are viewed as more valuable.

In a recent analysis of sales data from the Regional Multiple Listing Service (RMLS) in Portland, Oregon, certified green homes—that is, homes that were awarded third-party green certification (sort of like a green *Good Housekeeping* seal of approval)—sold for an average of $223 per square foot, while comparable standard homes sold for an average of $196 per square foot. In other terms, the green homes sold for 13.8% more per square foot than standard homes. The green homes also sold faster—one-third fewer days on the market.

Similar results were reported in Seattle. Of new homes built in 2007, those that had third-party green certifications sold in 18% less time than standard models. And sale prices were higher. The green homes, on average, were 25% smaller than comparables yet sold for 4% more, so priced per square foot, the green-certified homes were 37% more valuable. Green-certified condominiums in Seattle sold for 28% more per square foot than noncertified condos.

Owners of green homes clearly recognize the value they get from reduced utility expenses, improved indoor air quality and accompanying health benefits, and reduced maintenance costs associated with high-quality materials and durable construction methods. In a 2008 survey of residents of green-certified homes, 90% of respondents reported that they would choose a green home for their next place of residence, and most said they would pay more—80% said they would pay up to 5% more for a green home, while 36% said they would pay up to 10% more.

And if you should decide to sell your house one day, you will very likely get a better price for it. According to the Appraisal Institute (www.appraisalinstitute.org), an energy-efficient home can be valued $20 higher for every $1 in annual energy savings. That means that if your newly remodeled green home uses $1,000 less energy per year than a conventional home of the same size and comparable amenities, the value of your house just went up by $20,000.

In time, as more people begin to recognize the many other benefits of living in a green home, such as improved health and reduced maintenance, the market will place a monetary value on those things as well, making your green home even more valuable. But today many people already understand the concept that it is worth paying a little more for a house that will save them money every month because it uses less energy.

That is why I call energy efficiency the first fundamental of green remodeling. This is the fundamental that keeps on giving, because using less energy reduces environmental impacts such as climate change and air pollution, helps reduce our national dependence on foreign oil, and puts more money into our pockets every single month.

Placing a window close to a light-colored wall or ceiling (or both) can reflect more daylight into a room, reducing the number of hours you'll need to turn on the lights each day.

Improving energy efficiency through integrated design

There are so many strategies for making homes more energy efficient that it can be a little daunting to know where to begin. But it's a mistake to think of these strategies only in linear fashion, with a beginning and an end, because they are all interrelated. To achieve significant energy savings, it is necessary to consider all the parts of the house at once in a process known as *integrated design*.

In an integrated design process, we come to understand that everything affects everything else. Not only is the size of the heating, ventilation, and air-conditioning (HVAC) system related to the type of glazing in the windows and the amount of insulation in the walls, but also to the placement of the windows, the color of the walls, and even the type of curtains. What's that, you ask? Interior design affects the size of my air conditioner? Well, yes, it does. Here's why.

The heat produced by lightbulbs can be a significant factor in calculating a home's cooling loads. The number of light fixtures needed, and especially the number of hours they are on each day, has a lot to do with how much daylight is available inside the house. Placing windows close to a wall or ceiling, choosing window treatments that don't block the light, and painting adjacent surfaces a light color will reflect more daylight into the house. The more daylight you have, the fewer lights you'll need to turn on. If your house has plenty of natural light, you may never have to turn on the electric lights during the day at all, reducing the amount of heat generated by lightbulbs at the exact hours of the day when your air conditioner has to work the hardest.

Everything affects everything else, but we have to start somewhere. As I view it, there are five basic strategies for saving energy, which, especially when used in concert, can dramatically reduce the amount of energy consumed by any home.

For clarity, I have organized these five strategies in a logical order, as they can build on each other to achieve greater results. Remember, everything affects everything else. For example, it doesn't pay to spend money on more efficient mechanical equipment (strategy 2) before you do everything you can to reduce your home's demand for heating and cooling (strategy 1). If you do a good enough job of reducing demand with strategy 1, any new heating or air-conditioning system you might install as part of strategy 2 can be smaller and less expensive. Therefore, it will consume still less energy.

The strategies are also organized more or less in order of increasing complexity. None of it is exactly rocket science; you could probably do a lot of the things in strategy 1 yourself, if you were so inclined. But you are more likely to need help from a qualified professional as you move down the list.

▼◄ **From the exterior, you might think this house in Tennessee is just an ordinary 1970s ranch house with some solar panels stuck on the roof. But it is actually a net-zero energy home that uses numerous strategies to reduce energy consumption, which enables the solar panels on the roof to provide all the energy needed for running the house.**

▼▶ **Armed with a few tubes of caulk and a can of expanding foam, you can seal most air leaks in an average-size home in a few hours.**

Strategy 1: Reduce demand for heating and cooling

Very often when people call me to ask about how to make their home greener, the first thing they say is that they've been thinking about putting solar panels on their roof. It's a good thought but not the place to start. In fact, renewable energy is probably the last piece of the puzzle. There's no use in trying to figure out how much renewable energy you need to produce (either photo-voltaic, wind, or solar hot water) until you've done everything possible to reduce your home's demand for energy in the first place. So how do we do that?

Sealing air leaks Start with the obvious things. Ideally, your house should be as much like a thermos as possible. You want to create a tight thermal envelope to keep heat from escaping in winter and from entering the house in summer. Homes lose most of their heat through air movement. And most houses leak a lot of air. If you do nothing else to your home, the first and most important thing to do is to find air leaks and seal them with caulk, expanding foam, or weatherstripping.

Upgrading insulation Taking this to the next level, air sealing is ideally done in conjunction with beefing up your insulation. But insulation needs to be installed carefully to perform at its stated R-value. You thought you were getting R-19 walls because the roll of fiberglass insulation is marked R-19? Think again. In many homes, imperfectly installed insulation functions at only half its rated R-value.

Unless the insulation is installed perfectly (which in the real world is rare), there are often small gaps where two pieces of insulation meet, where the insulation gets stuffed behind a pipe or an electrical outlet, where it meets a window or door frame, or at the top of the wall if a piece is cut just a little short. All these little gaps, if added together, can be responsible for as much heat loss as leaving a window open.

To be truly effective, insulation must form a continuous barrier between conditioned spaces (finished living space that's heated and cooled) and unconditioned spaces (unfinished spaces, usually attics or basements). Small gaps make a big dent in the insulation's effectiveness. And there are several types of insulation to consider before making a choice (see chapter 4 for a discussion of all things insulation).

The original windows still found in many older homes are a major source of heat loss. Storm windows help some, but replacing old single-glazed windows with new, high-performing insulated units provides much better results with a good financial payback.

Replacing windows Windows represent the next chink in your home's thermal armor. While a well-insulated wall might be rated as R-19 or more, even the very best windows available from the major manufacturers have an equivalent insulating value of about R-3. And if you have old single-pane windows, those are closer to R-0. In either case, what this means is that you've got a lot of big holes in your house. There are a few things you can do about this, but it might not actually be the highest priority. Windows are expensive, and the value of the energy savings you can get from replacing them depends a lot on what kind of windows you are replacing—unless you have single-pane windows, in which case you really need to do something about it. They may keep the wind from blowing through your house, the value of which should not be entirely dismissed, but they don't do much else.

If new windows are not in your budget, you should at the very least check to see how much air infiltration you're getting through and around the window frame. You can observe this with a simple test. On a cold day, light a stick of incense and hold it close to a window or door. As you move it around, being careful not to set the drapes on fire, you will see from the movement of the smoke where you have drafts. If you see drafts around the outside of the frame, where the window trim meets the wall, you can easily seal that with a tube of caulk. (Use low-VOC caulk so that you're not filling your house with potentially harmful fumes as you seal the leaks. See chapter 8 for more details on nontoxic materials.)

If you see air movement where the window sash meets the frame, you might be able to replace the jamb liners or add weatherstripping. Better still would be to replace the old single-pane glass with new insulated window sash, if the budget permits. Weatherstripping can be done for just a few dollars per window if you do it yourself, but figure $35 to $50 for a professional job. New jamb liners might run you $75 to $125 per window. Replacing the window sash (the compete frame that holds the glass) runs anywhere from $300 to $800, depending on the size and type of window.

If you already have double-pane windows, though, especially if they are less than 12 years old, the amount of improvement you'd get by replacing them with new windows may be relatively small, unless you replace them with "super windows." While top-of-the-line windows from most of the major manufacturers have a thermal performance equivalent to R-3 at best, there are some super high-performance windows on the market today that achieve insulating values as high as R-11. These are more costly, to be sure, and the decision on whether they are worth the expense will depend on many factors, including your local climate, the size and number of windows in the house, which way they face, and, of course, your budget. But in many cases, super windows can pay for themselves in just a few years. Chapter 4 will go into more detail about windows.

Strategy 2: Use efficient mechanical systems

Once you have done as much as you can to reduce your home's demand for heating and cooling, the next strategy is to consider the efficiency of your heating and air-conditioning equipment. Efficiency ratings for all types of mechanical equipment have been going up in the past dozen years.

Combustion heating equipment is rated by its annual fuel utilization efficiency (AFUE), which represents the difference between the energy consumed and energy output. An AFUE of 80 means that 80% of the energy in the fuel becomes heat for the home and the other 20% escapes up the chimney. That does not take into account heat losses from leaky or uninsulated ductwork, or inefficiently designed ductwork with long runs, too much flex-duct, or too many elbows. Although older furnace and boiler systems had efficiencies in the range of 56% to 70%, modern conventional heating systems can achieve efficiencies as high as 97%, converting nearly all the fuel to useful heat for your home.

A smoke pencil, sometimes called a puffer stick or smoke stick, emits a small amount of nontoxic vapor that can help you find and eliminate unwanted air infiltration—a major cause of heat loss.

green view

Upgrading to a high-efficiency heating system can cut your fuel bills and your greenhouse gas emissions dramatically. According to the U.S. Department of Energy, upgrading your furnace or boiler from 56% to 90% efficiency in an average cold-climate house will save 1.5 tons of carbon dioxide emissions each year if you heat with gas or 2.5 tons if you heat with oil. And it would cut your fuel bill by nearly 40%.

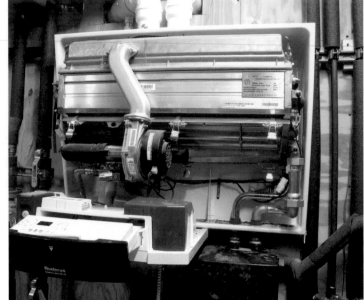

▲◀▶ Newer boilers, like this wall-hung model by Buderus, can be up to 97% efficient and take up much less space. Upgrading to a more efficient boiler can save you money and cut CO_2 emissions by more than two tons per year.

▶ Many old boilers send more than 40% of the energy they consume up the chimney. If a more efficient replacement is not in the budget, a tune-up can ensure that existing equipment performs as efficiently as possible.

Less is more In a well-insulated house, whatever kind of HVAC system you install can be smaller. In fact, not only *can* it be smaller, but you'll be asking for trouble if it isn't. Oversized heating and cooling equipment is much less efficient than "rightsized" systems because it will cycle on and off too quickly, failing to achieve its stated efficiency rating. This short cycling also causes more wear and tear on the equipment, which will need more frequent servicing and will wear out sooner.

Oversized equipment will also make your house less comfortable. In heating mode, the short cycling will result in drafts and hot and cold spots throughout the house. In AC mode, you'll get uneven cooling and poor dehumidification. With an oversized air conditioner, you need to make the house colder than you really want to get the unit to run long enough to bring the humidity down to comfortable levels.

In extremely well-insulated homes, especially those that employ additional energy-saving strategies like super windows and passive solar, you might not need a boiler at all. In some cases, a high-performance hot water heater can actually supply all the space heating you need.

Kicking the fossil fuel habit While modern gas- or oil-fired heating equipment can be quite efficient, it still burns fossil fuel. You would need to have been living in a cave for the last few years not to be aware of the damage that the burning of fossil fuels does to our environment *and* to our economy. Burning less of it is certainly preferable to burning more, but burning none would be a lot better. The architect William McDonnough, author of *Cradle to Cradle: Remaking the Way We Make Things,* often remarks that being less bad is not being good. It is being bad, only less so. So now let's take a look at being good instead of merely being less bad.

The great thing about electricity is that there are lots of ways to make it. Some of them are rather dirty, but in the coming decades more and more electricity will be from clean, renewable sources such as wind, solar, geothermal, small-scale hydroelectric, wave energy, and methane recaptured from landfills or from biomass. And as those technologies scale up, the price will come down.

Many experts now envision converting everything possible to electricity—cars, trucks, and trains, in addition to space and water heating. This, in conjunction with clean energy production, will be an important step toward a sustainable future. I'll go into greater detail on this in chapter 5, but for now let's take a brief look at two options.

In homes with a high-performing thermal envelope, the demand for heating is dramatically lower. In some cases, a boiler can be dispensed with altogether, and a high-efficiency hot water heater, like this model from A. O. Smith, supplies all the heat and domestic hot water the house needs.

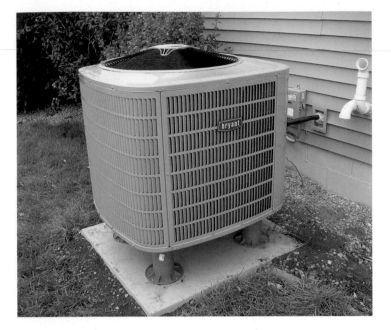

▲◄ **As the name implies, heat pumps move heat from one place to another. This air-source heat pump extracts ambient heat from the outdoors and uses it to heat your house.**

▲► **Ground-source or geothermal heat pumps circulate fluid through buried tubing, or draw water from a dedicated well, to extract energy stored in the earth, which can then be used for indoor space heating and water heating.**

▼ **The familiar blue Energy Star label tells you that a product meets or exceeds efficiency standards set by the U.S. Environmental Protection Agency.**

Air-source heat pumps A heat pump is basically a refrigerator running backwards. Everyone has had the experience of feeling warm air coming out of the bottom of the refrigerator. But did you ever stop to think where that warm air comes from? It comes from inside the refrigerator and the freezer where it's cold. Even air cold enough to keep ice frozen contains residual heat. To maintain the cold temperatures inside the refrigerator, it's necessary to continually pull residual heat out and put it someplace else. Just like a pump that moves water from one place to another, a heat pump moves heat from one place to another. (You can't eradicate heat. Heat is energy, and as you learned in school, energy cannot be created or destroyed. But it *can* be moved from one place to another.)

An air-source heat pump pulls heat out of the air outdoors and moves it to the inside of your house. And in the cooling season it runs backwards, pulling heat out of your house and putting it back outside. Heat pumps work most efficiently in warm to mild climates. If you live in a very cold climate, even though there is still some residual heat in the air that a heat pump could pump into your house, it has to work a lot harder to do it, which cuts into its efficiency.

Ground-source heat pumps Unlike air-source heat pumps, ground-source heat pumps, also known as water-source heat pumps or geothermal heat pumps, work just fine in cold climates. They extract heat from underground, where, even when the air outside is well below freezing for weeks at a time, the temperature stays relatively warm. Warmed by the earth's core, the temperature 6 ft. to 8 ft. below the surface never drops much lower than 50°F. From a heat pump's point of view, 50°F is toasty warm, plenty warm enough to heat your whole house.

Efficient appliances, like the Energy Star–rated laundry machines shown here, use a lot less water and electricity than standard models.

A switchable power strip can reduce phantom loads, sometimes called power vampires, by turning off things that draw current even when not in use.

Strategy 3: Reduce electrical demand

As a child, I never thought to wonder why my grandmother called the refrigerator "the ice box." I didn't realize then that, for her, an electric refrigerator was a fairly recent innovation. She had come of age in a world where people kept their food cool in an insulated box with a space for a large block of ice that would be delivered every few days by an iceman wielding an ungainly set of tongs. But since that time, the proliferation of electrically operated devices in the typical American home has grown exponentially.

If you were to add up all the electrical devices in your home, you would probably be shocked by the number of appliances, entertainment systems, computers, battery chargers, and other electrical conveniences we have come to depend on. We have also become accustomed to paying high electric bills that are getting higher all the time. What to do? If you're about to embark on a remodeling project, or even if you just want to reduce your electric bill, this is something you want to take a close look at.

Upgrading appliances Appliances are the largest consumers of watts in most homes, and the refrigerator is by far the hungriest, so let's start there. If you own a refrigerator that is more than 15 years old, it is gobbling up a hideous amount of current every day. New Energy Star®–rated refrigerators use a fraction as much electricity. They use so much less, in fact, that the savings to your electric bills will be enough to pay for a new, energy-efficient refrigerator in as little as three years.

Substantial savings can also be obtained with the newest generation of efficient dishwashers and laundry machines. These machines not only save electricity but also use far less water and detergent. It doesn't pay to rush right out and replace all the electronics in your house when you're remodeling, but when you do need something new, look for the Energy Star label on appliances, televisions, stereos, computers, and lots of other things as well. The savings will add up.

Phantom loads Not only do electrical devices use power when they are turned on, but many of them also use power even when they're turned off. According to the U.S. Department of Energy, 75% of the electricity used to power home electronics and appliances is consumed while the products are turned off. TVs, stereos, DVD players, and anything else that has a remote control or a clock or an indicator light continue to draw current 24 hours a day.

These phantom loads, or *power vampires,* as they are often called, pack a surprising wallop. By some estimates, up to 40% of the electricity consumed in the average home is used to power appliances when they're turned off. On a macro scale, phantom loads account for 6% of the total electricity used in the United States. On a micro scale, if you have 20 phantom loads in your house, it could be costing you $200 per year, according to Cornell University.

You can starve a lot of these vampires by simply unplugging things you're not using. Or, more convenient, plug these things into switchable power strips. These inexpensive devices make it a snap to cut off the juice from everything that doesn't absolutely need to be left on all the time.

Change your lightbulbs Lighting is the other big energy user. One-quarter of the electricity used in most homes goes for keeping the lights on. Cutting the amount of power used for lighting is without question the easiest and most cost-effective way to save electricity. Switching from incandescent bulbs, which are basically heating devices that happen to produce a little light as a by-product (95% of the power consumed by standard lightbulbs produces only heat), to long-lasting compact fluorescent bulbs (CFLs) is a quick and easy energy saver that will pay for itself in less than a year. (See the chart on p. 144 for a cost comparison of different types of lightbulbs.)

Strategy 4: Capture waste heat

The United States has been called the Saudi Arabia of waste heat. I won't go into much detail about this here—I have to save a few surprises for later chapters—but suffice it to say that we consume a lot of energy making hot air and hot water, and then we send it up the chimney or down the drain. We'll look at a few ways of capturing some of that waste heat in chapter 5.

STARVE POWER VAMPIRES (WITHOUT GETTING OUT OF BED)

As much as 75% of the electricity used by home electronics is consumed while they are not in use. Anything with a transformer or charger or any device that has a remote control or clock or glowing lights of any sort is drawing current even when the power switch is in the off position. These power vampires, as they have been called, are responsible for 6% of all the electricity use in the United States and can add 10% per month to your electricity bill.

What to do? The simplest solution is to plug such devices into switchable power strips that you can buy at any hardware store. In actual use, however, even if you do plug the TV in your bedroom into a power strip, you might not use it most of the time because that involves getting out of bed just as you're about to doze off for the night. Not even hard-core environmentalists relish doing that.

But during a remodeling project, you might well have the opportunity to implement a more elegant solution. You can ask your electrician to install switches that control specific outlets. If, for example, the outlet your TV, stereo, or whatever else might be drawing current in your bedroom were controlled by a switch right next to your bed, you'd be much more likely to turn it off at night. Instead of drawing current 24 hours a day, your TV would only use power for the time you actually spend watching television in bed.

For the do-it-yourselfer, there are over-the-counter remote-controlled outlet adapters that you can simply plug in wherever your power vampires lurk. A small, battery-powered remote switches them on and off.

THE HIGH COST OF CHEAP ENERGY

Everyone complains about the high cost of energy. But in reality it is both far more costly than we know, and, paradoxically, too cheap. The reason has to do with something called *externalities.* Let me explain by way of an analogy that I like to call "The Parable of Trash."

The Parable of Trash

Suppose you live in a big apartment house and the landlord doesn't want to pay for trash removal. Instead, all the trash gets piled up in an empty lot out back. The tenants don't complain because they like the fact that their rents are so affordable. And the empty lot is so big the tenants can't really see the trash from their windows. But eventually it begins to fill up, and trash starts blowing around and landing on the sidewalk in front of the building and in the park across the street. Not much, at first, but after a while the park is a mess and everyone walking down the street has to step over piles of garbage.

The town council could pass a law requiring building owners to clean up their own garbage, but the councilmen know this would lead to rent increases and people would complain. And it's an election year. Instead, the sanitation department puts its employees on overtime to keep up with the ever-increasing amounts of trash landing in the park.

Gradually, the overtime payments swell the town's budget deficit so much that property taxes go up. The tenants don't complain to their landlord about this. They know that the landlord doesn't set the town's tax rate. And even if they suspected a connection, they still wouldn't complain because they don't want to risk a rent increase. But they sure grumble about the high property taxes.

The Idea of Externalities

I use this analogy to explain the concept of externalities. An externality is an indirect result or effect that is not counted as a direct cost.

Coal-fired power plants have traditionally been thought to be the least expensive way to generate electricity. But burning coal is also very dirty. Burning coal pollutes the air and water and produces more greenhouse gas emissions per watt than any other fuel.

Even though our electric bills don't reflect it, global warming is already costing us a fortune and the costs are rising rapidly. These costs are being passed on to us in all sorts of ways, such as environmental cleanups, increased health-care costs, more expensive food and water, higher insurance premiums, and lower real estate values—not to mention military muscle devoted to protecting our access to supplies of foreign oil. None of these costs show up on our electric bills. They are considered externalities. Even though these external costs are a direct result of combusting fossil fuels, they are not calculated in the cost of producing and distributing electricity. But we end up paying for them all the same.

We allow ourselves to be deceived about the cost of externalities just as, in the analogy we looked at a moment ago, it didn't occur to us to blame the landlord for our high taxes. We know that generating electricity is a major cause of global warming, but we don't want our electric bills to go up. We'd rather someone else pays for the externalities. The problem is, that someone else is us.

The National Resources Defense Council (NRDC) estimates that the cost to American taxpayers of coping with climate change could exceed $270 billion annually by the year 2025 and more than $1 trillion a year by the end of the century. If those costs were fairly factored into our utility bills, the cost of energy from solar, wind, and other clean, renewable sources would suddenly become competitive.

Thomas Friedman, the Pulitzer Prize–winning author and *New York Times* columnist, writes that properly accounting for the cost of the externalities associated with burning fossil fuels would set a price signal that would trigger vast amounts of ingenuity and capital investment in clean energy, which would create millions of jobs, grow our economy, reduce our dependence on unfriendly oil-producing nations, prevent the most catastrophic effects of climate change, and inspire the rest of the world to follow our lead.

The amount of solar energy hitting the earth every hour is greater than all the energy used in a year by everyone on the planet. It's just falling from the sky. All we have to do is level the playing field so that it becomes profitable to pick it up. Imagine if dollar bills were falling from the sky. Would

The cost of environmental damage from burning fossil fuels doesn't show up on our electric bills, but we pay for it in other ways.

you be satisfied if one or two occasionally landed in your pocket? Or would you buy a butterfly net? And how many of your neighbors would be out tinkering in the garage, inventing bigger and better nets?

Recognizing the true cost of producing "cheap" energy from fossil fuels will catapult us into a future of clean, reliable, and affordable energy. It will cost some money to make that happen, but it will cost vastly more not to.

Every day, enough free solar energy falls on the earth to supply all of our energy needs for a year. Rooftop solar panels, such as the photovoltaic panels and solar hot water collectors shown here, provide homes with a virtually endless supply of clean, renewable energy.

Strategy 5: Harvest free energy

Now we can talk about solar panels. Once we've done all we can to reduce demand by conserving energy, tightening up the home's thermal envelope, and installing efficient mechanical systems, we finally have an idea of how much energy we really need to supply our newly energy-efficient home. So now we can consider where we can get it for free.

Actually, the energy is free, but the getting of it is not. Solar panels and wind turbines are expensive, but they are becoming cheaper all the time. The problem is mainly one of scale. When popular demand, necessity, and government incentives grow the market for photovoltaic (PV) panels, solar water heaters, wind turbines, and other renewable energy sources, the price will drop and clean energy will be as cheap as or cheaper than dirty energy.

If you'd like to include renewable energy generation as part of your green remodel, the most common methods of producing renewable energy for your home are solar hot water, PV solar panels, and small wind turbines. You need to live in a fairly windy location, with annual wind speeds averaging 10 mph to 12 mph, for wind to be a practical option. Solar panels are practical in more locales because the sun shines everywhere. The main consideration for most homeowners contemplating some form of solar panels is having an unobstructed spot to place them—ideally a piece of south-facing roof that isn't in the shadow of trees or other buildings. If you don't have a south-facing roof but do have a sunny yard, a ground-based solar array is also possible. We'll take a closer look at renewable energy options in chapter 6.

FUNDAMENTAL 2: RESOURCE EFFICIENCY

You turn on the tap and water comes out. Every time. Simple, yes? Well, not as simple as it once was. Water shortages are cropping up all over the country and becoming acute in many areas. We have grown used to hearing about water shortages out west in arid parts of the country. But today water shortages are being felt in many more places.

Georgia, once amply supplied with water, recently experienced such severe shortages that the governor declared a state of emergency for the northern third of the state and asked the White House to declare it a major disaster area. And water shortages in Georgia carry the potential of serious consequences for Florida, its downstream neighbor. The desert is no longer the only region of this country that is chronically thirsty.

Water utilities around the country are struggling to come up with enough water to meet the growing demand. Some areas have adopted variable pricing models that charge consumers higher rates for water use beyond a prescribed amount in order to discourage high water use. Necessity has bred a variety of creative water-conservation programs. Several water districts have started giving high-efficiency toilets to their customers at no charge. The reason is that it is far less expensive to pay people to conserve water than it is to build new reservoirs, pipelines, water-treatment facilities, and wastewater-treatment plants. In southern Nevada, an area with particularly acute water shortages, the local water authority pays customers up to $1.50 per square foot to replace their lawns with low-water-use, drought-tolerant landscaping.

Remodeling is the perfect time to find ways to cut your water use. But can reducing your personal water use possibly have any impact on water shortages? Absolutely. There are a whole lot of houses in this country, and each one uses a lot of water. Let's look at a few practical examples of how much water a green remodel can save.

Too precious to waste: Severe water shortages in every part of the world make conservation measures an essential element of green remodeling.

Money down the drain

In the early 1980s, government mandates for water conservation required the plumbing industry to switch from 5-gallons-per-flush (gpf) toilets to 3.5 gpf. Boy, did people complain. Clogs were common and a lot of people found they had to flush twice, which, needless to say, didn't help the cause of conservation much. But toilet design improved and complaints died down. That is, until 1996 when new federal regulations mandated 1.6-gpf toilets. Once again, it took a while for function to catch up with the mandate.

Today, there is a new generation of toilets that require only 1.28 gpf, and some models use less than a gallon. These new high-efficiency toilets (HETs) actually work extremely well and can save a lot of water. HETs use at least 20% less water than 1.6-gpf models.

Big savings flow from low-flow showerheads

Early water-saving showerheads that surfaced in the 1980s were rather anemic. People still wince when the subject comes up. But the technology has improved so much that you can experience a completely satisfying shower using a fraction as much water. If you like to sing in the shower, "Pennies from

green view

If you replace a 3.5-gpf toilet with a 1.28-gpf high-efficiency toilet, assuming there are four people in your household, you'll save about 10,000 gallons of water per year. Depending on water and sewer rates where you live, a high-efficiency toilet could pay for itself in four to six years. And it could be much less than that because many older toilets leak. A worn flapper valve can waste 2 gallons per minute. If you are replacing a toilet that runs an extra 30 minutes a day, your new high-efficiency toilet could pay for itself in a year.

Water-efficient plumbing fixtures, like the 1.5-gallon-per-minute faucets shown here, not only save water but also the energy used for water heating.

Heaven" or "We're in the Money" might be good choices because big savings flow from low-flow showerheads. I'll go into more detail in chapter 6, but between the water saved and the savings in water-heating energy costs, a family of four can save hundreds of dollars a year—possibly as much as $1,000—by switching to efficient showerheads.

No matter what part of the house your remodel touches, it certainly makes sense to replace your showerheads while you're at it, even if you touched nothing else in any bathroom.

The savings scale up

How, you might ask, can my small remodeling project have an impact on the global water crisis? As I've said before, there are a lot of houses in this country. Low-flow toilets, for example, can save a family of four more than 10,000 gallons of water per year. If one-quarter of the 100 million or so households in this country switched to low-flow toilets, that would save 250 billion gallons of water per year. If the same number of households switched to low-flow showerheads, it would save more than 430 billion gallons per year. Low-flow faucets in those same households would save another 200 billion gallons or so, and efficient washing machines and dishwashers would save another 156 billion gallons. That's more than 1 trillion gallons of water—more than the total annual consumption of New York, Chicago, and Los Angeles—that could be saved each year from just a quarter of U.S. households switching to more efficient toilets, faucets, showerheads, and appliances.

Conserving lumber

What about other resources, like trees, for example? The average new home consumes two to three acres of timber in its construction. And a lot of that lumber ends up in the Dumpster® through poor planning and wasteful construction practices. It has been estimated that for every six new homes built, the amount of wasted lumber would be enough to build one more house of the same size.

Remodeling homes uses a lot less lumber than building new ones, but there are ways we could use still less—not only in more efficient use of new lumber but also in finding ways to re-use lumber reclaimed as parts of a structure are dismantled. There are many ways to conserve virgin materials when you remodel. In chapter 7 we'll look at a variety of reclaimed materials, rapidly renewable materials, and products and materials with recycled content, as well as construction methods that conserve lumber.

FUNDAMENTAL 3: HEALTHY LIVING ENVIRONMENTS

We feel safe inside our homes. Inside, we are protected from rain, wind, snow, and excessive heat or cold. But do our homes also protect our health? Sadly, the air inside a great many homes contains far higher levels of pollutants than outdoor air. In some homes, the air is a hundred times more polluted. When did our homes become so toxic?

The oil embargoes of the 1970s prompted millions of homeowners to better insulate their houses—primarily with fiberglass insulation that contained formaldehyde. Around the same time, central air-conditioning was becoming the norm rather than the exception, changing from a luxury to a necessity in public perception.

Many new building materials were coming into wide use at that time, too. Plywood, made with formaldehyde-based adhesives, had been increasingly used in homebuilding since the 1950s, but homes then were not well insulated and thus always had plenty of fresh air. Plastics were also growing in popularity, as were synthetic carpeting and vinyl flooring and wall coverings. Adhesives containing volatile organic compounds (VOCs) were also coming into wide use in homebuilding. And let's not forget about asbestos.

These stair treads from LEED (Leadership in Energy and Environmental Design) Platinum home in Michigan were made from beams that the contractor salvaged while renovating an old theater a few blocks away.

Eliminating pollution-trapping materials like heavy draperies and wall-to-wall carpeting helps minimize exposure to allergens and irritants such as pollen, mold spores, dust mites, and pet dander. Use low-VOC paints and finishes to further ensure a healthy living environment.

By the end of the 1970s, new homes were routinely built much tighter than their predecessors in an effort to conserve energy, but also with the routine addition of central air-conditioning, which had the opposite effect on energy costs. More and more people started living in hermetically sealed homes built with dozens of new materials that ranged from slightly toxic to downright deadly, and with climate-control systems that continuously recirculated the indoor air.

Asthma and allergy rates, which have a known link to airborne pollutants, have more than doubled from 1980 to the present. And many other illnesses that were almost unheard of 30 years ago are now known or are suspected to be linked to environmental factors. Does anyone notice a pattern emerging here?

Fortunately, building science is much better understood now than it was a few decades ago, and we know a lot more about how to build homes that won't make us sick. There are three important strategies to keep in mind for creating healthy living spaces:

- Pollutant source control: Avoid building materials with unhealthy ingredients.
- Humidity control: Excess humidity breeds mold and dust mites, two powerful allergens.
- Ventilation and filtration.

Build tight and ventilate right

A phrase used repeatedly in discussions of green building is "build tight and ventilate right." Older homes were so drafty they never had air-quality problems—there was always plenty of fresh air. But we need tightly built homes to conserve energy, so we need some type of mechanical ventilation to provide the fresh air we need. And while we're bringing in that fresh air, we have the opportunity to filter out all kinds of airborne pollutants. With proper attention to these three strategies for healthy indoor environmental quality, we can have homes that are both extremely energy efficient and extremely healthy to live in. Chapter 8 will cover occupant health and indoor air quality in depth.

Now that we've taken a brief look at the three fundamentals of green building and remodeling, along with a sampling of strategies for implementing them, we're ready to delve more deeply into each of them. In the chapters that follow, we'll see examples of how all these strategies have been employed with boundless resourcefulness and creativity to produce revitalized, recycled homes that are at once beautiful, efficient, healthy, and environmentally responsible.

GREEN REMODEL

EXPANDING UP AND DOWN IN SEATTLE

Unlike the other homes profiled throughout this book, this green remodel of a small 1921 house in Seattle's Phinney Ridge neighborhood was not created for a particular homeowner. Rather, it was built on spec by the architect and a former client who wanted to put their convictions about green design and construction to the test. The completed house, which nicely illustrates all three fundamentals of green remodeling—energy efficiency, a healthy living environment, and efficient use of resources—sold within three days of hitting the market.

The plan (or "program") for the house called for adding a second floor and creating additional living space on the basement level without enlarging the foundation. Although the completed home offers more than twice the living space of the original, the energy bills are $500 lower per year than for the original home.

Raising the first floor by 12 in. turned the cramped, dark basement into warm, comfortable living space for a bedroom/office, bathroom, and playroom with ample daylight from a glass door and new windows. Additional daylight filters in from the first floor due to a relocated stair with open risers. PEX tubing embedded in a new floor slab of concrete mixed with fly ash makes the basement level feel dry and cozy even on the coldest days.

A range of sustainable materials makes the house both healthy to live in and easy on the environment.

PROJECT AT A GLANCE

Originally built: 1921

Original size: 1,880 sq. ft.

Size after remodel: 2,830 sq. ft.

Architect: Jim Burton, Blip Design

Contractor: Jim Burton/Jeff Lewis

The first floor was reconfigured by the elimination of walls, turning several small rooms into an open, airy living space.

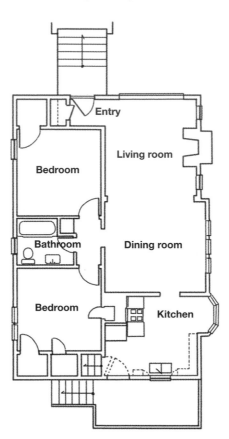

FIRST FLOOR (BEFORE)

Entry
Living room
Bedroom
Bathroom
Dining room
Bedroom
Kitchen

FIRST FLOOR (AFTER)

Entry
Closet
Living room
Bathroom
Dining room
Den
Kitchen
Deck

BEFORE　　AFTER

ENERGY EFFICIENCY

Heat is supplied by a new, high-efficiency gas boiler and distributed by radiant flooring on all three levels. For the two upper floors, plywood subflooring with an aluminum surface spreads the heat evenly. The panels come with grooves specially designed to receive the PEX hot-water tubing.

A tightly sealed thermal envelope keeps the heat in. Prior to insulating, a blower door test was performed to discover potential air leaks (see "Conducting an Energy Audit" on p. 229), which were then sealed with expanding foam. Airtight drywall construction further ensures minimal air infiltration. Then the exterior was wrapped with 1-in. rigid foam insulation to eliminate thermal bridging and increase the total R-value of the wall assembly. Efficient lighting and appliances also reduce energy usage.

▲◄ Low-VOC paint in a crisp color palette enlivens the interior and defines various functions within the open floor plan. The flooring is wheatboard.

▲▶ A new stair with open risers allows daylight from a tall front window to filter into all three levels.

◄ The remodel more than doubled the living space of the original cottage without any expansion of the home's footprint. By expanding up, rather than out, the foundation and most of the first floor were essentially recycled, conserving resources and keeping costs down.

▲ The open kitchen features Energy Star appliances and a quintet of sustainable materials: natural linoleum flooring, wheatboard cabinets with an FSC-certified hardwood veneer, and PaperStone™ countertops made from recycled paper. The structural beam is made from reclaimed lumber.

▶ Exterior porches feature Ipe decking over a structure of galvanized steel, which is maintenance-free and can be recycled at the end of its useful life.

A HEALTHY LIVING ENVIRONMENT

Multiple strategies ensure excellent indoor air quality. The bare floors deny indoor pollutants, such as pollen, dust mites, and mold spores, a place to hide. Low-emitting materials and finishes throughout the house eliminate another source of indoor air pollution—off-gassing of toxic compounds. And an energy-recover ventilator (ERV) equipped with high-efficiency air filters continuously supplies the tightly sealed interior with fresh, clean air.

EFFICIENT USE OF RESOURCES

Rapidly renewable materials, reclaimed materials, and materials with recycled content were all chosen to help conserve natural resources. The new second floor was framed using Forest Stewardship Council (FSC)-certified lumber, and an exposed structural beam on the first floor is made from reclaimed lumber. Wheatboard, made from agricultural waste, is used both as flooring, with a zero-VOC finish, and for the kitchen cabinets with an FSC-certified hardwood veneer. The kitchen flooring is Marmoleum®, made from wood flour and linseed oil, with natural jute backing.

On the exterior, the house features an unusual and extremely durable siding detail. Sustainably harvested Ipe wood is installed with stainless-steel fasteners over the rigid insulation and a rain screen—a waterproof barrier that comes in rolls (see chapter 7). Furring strips create a gap between the siding and the rain screen, promoting drainage for any accumulation of moisture, and an air space that allows the siding to breathe. Ipe can be finished with a vegetable-derived oil to preserve the original, natural color. Left unfinished, it will weather to a soft silver-gray.

* Efficient space planning more than doubles the living space without expanding the home's footprint.

* Construction debris was recycled (wood, metals, carpets, cabinets, plumbing fixtures, even the front door).

* The tightly sealed and well-insulated shell minimizes heat loss.

* Energy-efficient lighting, appliances, and heating keep utility bills low.

* Low-emitting materials and fresh, filtered air provide top-notch indoor environmental quality.

* Reclaimed, recycled, and renewable materials conserve natural resources.

* Native and drought-resistant landscaping conserves water.

* Durable, low-maintenance materials reduce future repairs, saving money, energy, and natural resources.

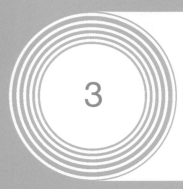

3 GREEN BY DESIGN

What do green homes look like? Can you tell if a home is green by its appearance? Does remodeling green require changing the style of your home in ways that might not appeal to you? Will using healthy, sustainable materials recall the look of a 1960s-era commune? If you are considering a green remodel, these might be some of the first questions that pop into your mind. After all, you want your home to look like, well, your home—not like something that landed in the neighborhood from another planet. Let me put your mind at rest.

Without question, many of the sustainable features of green remodels pictured in this book are the result of careful design. Yet, in every case, the appearance of these homes is entirely a function of the owner's taste and the architect's imagination. Designing green is more about function than appearance—the way a house responds to its physical environment (to the variables of place and climate) and the way various parts of the house relate to each other.

◄ Any style house can be green. While totally different in scale, budget, and appearance, each of these homes was remodeled with sustainability in mind, making them more energy efficient, environmentally friendly, and healthier to live in.

▶ Each year more than 350,000 homes are torn down to make way for new ones.

GOOD DESIGN IS SUSTAINABLE DESIGN

Remodeling is green by nature. The essence of remodeling means extending the useful life of a structure—in other words, recycling your whole house (or most of it). But when houses become obsolete they end up in landfills. Every year, more than 350,000 homes in the United States are demolished, rather than remodeled, to make way for new ones. The resulting waste, burden to landfills, and subsequent materials and energy required for new homes on those sites place an increasingly untenable strain on the earth's natural resources.

We can get some clues about this by looking at old houses. It is tempting to think that older houses were always better designed than ones of more recent vintage. But that is only partly true. Where I live in Connecticut, the hills are fairly dotted with beautiful old colonials anywhere from 100 to 200 years old or more—sometimes much more. But it may be that the reason we think older houses were so uniformly well designed is that the poor ones didn't last. Perhaps it is only the ones generations of owners cherished for their beauty and utility that have been lovingly maintained over time, enabling them to survive to the present day. The clunkers were all long since torn down.

That is not to cast aspersions on modern design. Any style house can be beautiful. What the best modern houses have in common with old houses are fine proportions, human scale, warmth of spirit, and convenient layouts. Without these qualities, houses eventually end up at the dump.

GREEN IS NOT A STYLE

The first lesson of green design is that it has little or nothing to do with the architectural style of your house. Whether your home is contemporary or classical, a Georgian colonial or a shingled Queen Anne, an adobe Pueblo Revival or a Craftsman bungalow, whether you are planning a modest addition or an extreme makeover, you can incorporate green principles to make your home more comfortable, energy efficient, environmentally responsible, and healthier to live in.

While less a matter of style than function, many green strategies can and should influence the way you approach designing a remodeling project. Ideas such as providing for better daylighting and natural ventilation or adding building elements that prevent excessive solar gain in summer but admit the sun's light and warmth in winter can, with a little thought, be accomplished within the architectural vocabulary of any given style. I'll show you many examples of this throughout the book.

Good design is sustainable. Many fine old homes dating back to colonial times have been lovingly preserved by generations of owners because of their timeless style and proportions. Forms that retain their appeal after hundreds of years tend not to end up in landfills.

UNDERSTANDING THE ELEMENTS OF GOOD DESIGN

It would be a dreary world, indeed, if we all had exactly the same notion of what a house should look like. But opinion is pretty unanimous about what we want our houses to *feel* like. We want them to feel like home. When we pull into the driveway or saunter up the front walk or step out of the elevator, what we want is a sense of place that is uniquely ours—welcoming, nurturing, safe, familiar. Ideally, optimists that we all are at heart, we would like our houses to make us feel good each time we arrive at home.

This is not a novel idea. In the first century AD, the Roman architect Vitruvius wrote that buildings should embody three qualities—*firmitas, utilitas*, and *venustas*. The first two of these, *firmitas* and *utilitas*, refer to a building's durability and functionality—will it hold up over time, and does it serve the purpose for which it was intended? The third, *venustas*, which Vitruvius considered equally important, can be defined as a sense of beauty or delight.

But what does a *green* home look like? Or perhaps a better question is, what should a green home look like? We might even start with a simpler question: What do we want our homes to look like? What does it take to delight us these days? It was the architect Louis Sullivan who famously stated, "It is the pervading law of all things . . . that form ever follows function." In other words, a building's appearance, he believed, should reflect its purpose. In that context, we might start by asking, what purpose do our homes serve? What is their function? And do green homes serve any different purpose than other homes? My short answer to that question would be that a green home serves exactly the same purpose as a conventionally built home but that it functions better. And some of the ways in which it functions better might even serve to provide additional v*enustas,* or delight.

The purpose of a green home, after all, is not to be green but to provide all the functions and benefits we expect of any building we call home—though in a more efficient, healthful, and sustainable manner.

Design and function

On the most basic level, a home provides shelter. It protects us from the elements: It keeps us warm in winter, cool in summer, and dry when it rains; keeps out bugs, wild animals, and other intruders; and grants us a measure of privacy. We also expect our homes to provide space for the way we live, for fostering relationships with loved ones, raising a family, preparing food, entertaining friends, and pursuing our hobbies. Many of us now work from home at least part of

the time. This is a relatively new phenomenon in the history of houses, but increasingly we need some part of the home to function as an office. That's a lot to expect of one structure, but somehow most homes do manage to do most of those things, if occasionally imperfectly.

But what portion of the world's natural resources is it reasonable for one house to consume to provide those functions? And when considering the protective functions of a home, does it occur to us to ask how well it protects our health? Is the air inside safe to breathe? Are we being exposed to harmful chemical compounds or unhealthy levels of allergens such as dust, pollen, and mold spores? (I'll cover all that in detail in chapter 8.) And should we stop to ask if the house is protecting our financial well-being? What portion of our own resources will be required to maintain the house and—especially in an age of escalating energy costs—to heat and cool it, to run the appliances, and to keep the lights on?

DESIGNING FOR THE LONG HAUL: DURABILITY IS GREEN

Just as remodeling an existing house extends its useful life and prevents entire structures from ending up in landfills, there are other steps we can take while remodeling to reduce the strain on our planet's resources. As we will see, remodeling in ways that reduce maintenance and increase a home's durability is very green indeed.

Each year, billions of dollars are spent on home repairs—repainting, reroofing, and replacing siding, trim, mechanical systems, and much else that has worn out or become obsolete. This

▲◀ *Utilitas:* Efficient space planning allows multiple functions to coexist, packing the most **functionality** into the limited space of this remodeled Portland, Maine, loft.

▲▲ *Venustas:* A cozy window seat adds a sense of **delight** to this naturally ventilated ranch house remodel in Orinda, California.

▲ *Firmitas:* Low-maintenance materials, such as fiber cement siding and Ipe wood sun shades, add to the **durability** of this St. Paul, Minnesota, home.

Durable and low-maintenance materials, such as expanded PVC trim and composite columns, reduce a home's life-cycle carbon footprint due to the energy and materials that won't be consumed by future repairs. On this house, the paint manufacturer's limited lifetime warranty claims the home's exterior will never need repainting, further reducing the quantity of natural resources ordinarily consumed by home repair and maintenance.

impacts our environment in many ways, but two stand out: waste disposal and the continuous need for manufacturing and installing a multitude of products and materials.

Every product, appliance, and building material used in home repairs starts out as raw materials that must be harvested or extracted from the earth. These include not only trees but also mineral resources such as copper, steel, aluminum, gypsum, and petroleum—lots and lots of petroleum. A fantastic variety of materials used in home construction, repair, and furnishing are made from petroleum by-products: paints and finishes, adhesives, insulation, roofing, siding, floor and wall coverings—the list goes on and on. And then there's the fuel consumed in transporting building materials, which brings us to the concept of embodied energy.

Embodied energy

Embodied energy is the sum total of all the energy expended in creating, delivering, and installing any material or product. This includes the fuel consumed in extracting raw materials from the earth, transporting them to manufacturing facilities, distributing the finished products to suppliers, delivering them to the job site, and then installing them. Swinging a hammer may not look like it requires the combustion of fossil fuel, but the carpenter had to drive to the job site, and someone had to go pick up coffee and donuts for the crew. And it took energy to manufacture that hammer, to say nothing of the electricity used by power tools, plus the energy it takes to manufacture, deliver, and maintain them.

The associated transportation costs alone consume a staggering amount of fuel and produce correspondingly vast quantities of greenhouse gases. Just think of all the millions of individual trips to home centers and hardware stores that are generated each year by the need for basic home repairs and maintenance.

This adds up to a lot of energy required for even the most basic home maintenance or repair, with all the attendant pollution and greenhouse gas emissions—much more than most of us have ever imagined. And then, whatever was being replaced ends up in an overburdened landfill, along with the construction waste and the packaging from the new materials.

HOW MUCH SPACE DO YOU REALLY NEED?

The easiest way to build or remodel green is quite simply to build smaller. Most Americans seem to want more and more space, but this trend, as we'll see, is not sustainable. Large houses consume a lot of everything, from water to lumber to copper and steel to the wide range of petroleum-derived materials we discussed above. And they require lots of energy to keep them warm in winter and cool in summer.

How can the earth's resources of water, raw materials, and fossil fuels keep up with the housing demands of a rapidly growing population? If the earth has a finite amount of natural resources, which clearly it does, and each year we keep using up those resources faster than we did the year before, which we surely are doing, that is not something that can be sustained indefinitely. Lest we go the way of the dinosaurs, we must find ways to use our planet's natural resources more sparingly. Building smaller is one way to get there.

Small is green. With thoughtful design and efficient space planning, we can remodel our homes to comfortably meet our needs in less space than we might assume, conserving materials and energy and saving money in the process. The master suite addition to this Texas bungalow was designed to expand the home's footprint as little as possible.

HOW MUCH GAS DOES IT TAKE TO MAINTAIN YOUR HOUSE?

Repairing and maintaining our homes entails a lot of driving back and forth to hardward stores and home centers. By looking at sales figures we can estimate that this activity alone accounts for roughly 40 million miles of driving per day, or more than 14 billion miles per year—roughly equal to 61,000 round trips to the moon.

The average car on the road today gets 17 miles to the gallon, which means that nearly 3 million gallons of gas are burned every day, just from contractors and do-it-yourselfers picking up home improvement materials.

Each gallon of gasoline burned in an internal combustion engine releases approximately 1.5 lbs of carbon dioxide into the atmosphere. That comes to a little over 3.5 million lbs of CO_2 per day, more than 70 million metric tons per year, just from home improvement–related driving.

Durability is an importnat aspect of building green. Long-lasting materials and construction details that help a home resist the ravages of time can reduce the amount of building materials that eventually need to be replaced, reduce the amount of time spent in the car, and increase the amount of time we spend enjoying our homes. And we just might help save the planet in the process.

SMALL IS GREEN: MAKING THE MOST OF AVAILABLE SPACE

When the owners of this house in Connecticut decided to remodel, the constraints of their lot ruled out any sizeable addition. Working with the same architect who had designed the house for them 15 years earlier, they reconfigured the interior to squeeze more function out of the limited space they had to work with. A two-story living room gave up some of its height to insert a loft space above that functions as a study. The loft, which reaches up into the rafters for its headroom, still allowed for an 11-ft. ceiling height in the living room below. And a flexible first-floor plan now allows for multiple uses of the same space.

The only addition to the home's footprint was a 125-sq.-ft. mudroom. The loft added 315 sq. ft. of living space without expanding either the footprint or the HVAC system. And a stair landing that was turned into a library nook provided another 36 sq. ft. of functional space that had previously been used only for circulation.

While increasing the lot coverage by just 125 sq. ft., the home's functional living space increased 476 sq. ft., going from 2,424 sq. ft. to 2,900 sq. ft.

▲ The study was carved out of the upper part of a double-height living room, creating more living space without enlarging the home's footprint. The extra square footage was created with a fraction of the building materials an addition would have consumed and didn't require enlarging the HVAC system.

▶ An 11-ft. ceiling creates drama in this small living room, while the oversized windows flood the space with sunlight, making it feel spacious and airy.

The built-in bookcases and window seat turned this stair landing into a library nook, adding new functionality to existing space. The large window brings daylight into both the first- and second-floor hallways.

Making less equal more

Our perception of space is elastic, influenced by many more things than just the shape and dimensions of a room. With thoughtful design, smaller spaces can be made to feel generous. Scale, proportion, ceiling height, the placement of doors and windows, views, light, and color all play a role in making the most of smaller spaces.

Scale is the relationship of architectural space to human dimensions. Proportion is the relationship of one element in a room to another. In the hands of a talented designer, these tools can be manipulated to make any home feel gracious and commodious, regardless of its size. But without careful attention to scale and proportion, even very large homes can seem inhospitable and lacking in useful, comfortable spaces.

Varying ceiling heights and the dimensions of transitional spaces can also be employed to enhance our perception of space and volume. Passing through a small, compressed space, such as a vestibule or hallway with a deliberately lowered ceiling, makes the adjacent room feel larger. Creating a variety of such transitions from one space to another adds drama and visual interest that can often make smaller homes feel quite grand.

green view

Many homes built during the 1980s and '90s featured double-height spaces intended to create a sense of drama. In most cases, though, they only served to make the rooms feel cold and inhospitable. Capturing some of that wasted volume is a green remodeling strategy that creates usable space out of thin air.

Design strategies such as placement of windows and doors to extend sight lines, open space planning, and even the use of color can make modest-size homes feel spacious.

Higher than normal ceilings, where the opportunity presents itself, also make rooms feel larger. Each additional foot overhead increases our perception of a room's horizontal dimensions by 2 ft. This effect can be increased by placing windows close to the ceiling or near adjacent light-colored walls. The light reflected off these surfaces makes a room feel bright, spacious, and airy.

Aligning windows and doors to create long axial views also enhances our perception of space and allows borrowed light from one room to brighten up another. Views from one room, through another, and out a window or to some other focal point also serve to make smaller spaces feel generous, as the room's occupants never feel closed in.

Eliminating wasted space and creating efficient floor plans also serve to make less equal more. Cutting down on unnecessary circulation and finding ways to allow the same space to serve multiple functions can pack much more utility into the spaces we do build and remodel. A stair landing can become a library nook with built-in bookshelves and a cozy place to sit and read. One corner of a kitchen can double as a home office. And open floor plans can provide added flexibility and functionality without increasing a home's footprint.

Plan ahead for flexibility. Sometimes a small change like relocating a window or doorway makes it easier for a room to multitask. Instead of devoting space to a formal dining room used only on special occasions, a living room or family room designed with flexibility in mind can accommodate a sit-down Thanksgiving dinner for the whole extended family.

Narrow clerestory windows placed high in the wall of this California master bedroom illuminate the room with reflected light and give the space a visual lift, creating the impression of a higher ceiling.

WORKING WITH NATURE: THE BEST THINGS IN GREEN ARE FREE

Good design can make our homes more sustainable in other ways, too. With careful thought and planning, some of the greatest benefits of green remodeling can be had essentially for free or for a small incremental cost. When planning a remodel, it doesn't cost us anything to stop for a moment and notice which direction the sun is coming from and which way the prevailing breezes blow. Once we know those things, we can make use of them.

Natural ventilation

Many people find themselves running the air-conditioning even on days when the temperature outdoors is perfectly comfortable. The problem they're trying to overcome is not so much excessive heat but stagnant air. Indoor air can be stagnant even with all the windows open if they are not optimally placed for good cross-ventilation. But when planning a renovation, it is often possible to align windows on opposite sides of a room. Aligning them on opposite sides of the house will work, too, if there are open passageways between rooms. And if you know which direction the prevailing wind comes from, you can go one step further and plan your renovation to capture pleasant breezes simply by putting openings in their path.

In the absence of windows on opposite sides of a room, operable units on two adjacent walls can also provide good passive ventilation.

We can learn a lot about natural ventilation from looking at old houses. Although it became something of a lost art, many homes were built to promote natural cooling, long before the invention of air-conditioning. They were cold and drafty in winter, with little or no insulation, but people coped by wearing heavy clothing. In summer, though, our fore-

LINING UP THE OPENINGS

Aligning windows and doorways on a long axis visually opens up smaller spaces, creates drama by framing views with a series of openings, brings daylight into the home's interior, and promotes good cross-ventilation, which can reduce cooling costs.

BEFORE

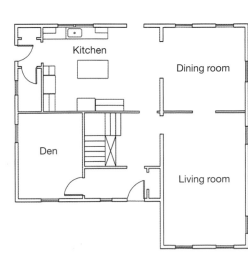

AFTER

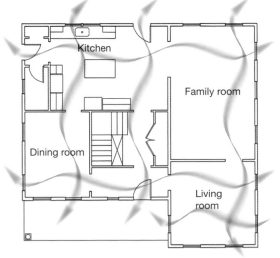

SHOTGUN VENTILATION

Architectural styles in warm climates have historically evolved with features designed to keep homes cool. The green restoration of this New Orleans shotgun cottage damaged in Hurricane Katrina preserves the feature that gave the style its name. Aligning all of the interior doors with windows at either end of these long, narrow houses, such that a bullet fired from the street could pass all the way through to the backyard, promotes the unimpeded flow of cooling breezes. Even with the doors closed, operable transoms could still provide good ventilation.

KEEPING COOL WITHOUT AIR-CONDITIONING

This green remodel in Seattle incorporates passive stack ventilation to keep the interior comfortable without the use of air-conditioning. Cool air is drawn in through ground-level windows as the more buoyant warm air exits naturally through the cupola. An open stairway acts as a chimney that permits natural convection currents to keep the air moving. Atop the cupola, a canopy of solar panels that provide clean, renewable electricity and hot water is positioned to shade the interior from the heat of the summer sun while allowing winter sunlight to brighten the home's interior.

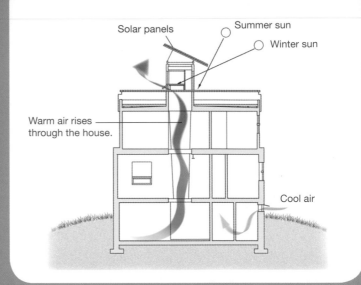

Solar panels

Summer sun

Winter sun

Warm air rises through the house.

Cool air

Operable transoms, like the ones in this remodeled home in Austin, Texas, promote natural ventilation without sacrificing privacy.

bears weren't inclined, as we are today, to keep cool by going around in shorts, tee shirts, and flip-flops, even in the privacy of their own homes. Placing windows for good cross-ventilation was one common technique. Operable louvered shutters were another, employed to block the sun's heat while still admitting cooling breezes. Homeowners then were aware of the path of the sun and the direction of the wind and would open or close the shutters on different sides of the house at different times of day in response to those predictable natural cycles.

Many homes also had cupolas that served the dual function of bringing light into the center of the house and pulling hot air out. On summer days, opening first-floor windows a few inches could produce a highly effective convection current. Warm air is less dense than cooler air, which makes it buoyant (remember the Wizard of Oz floating away in his hot-air balloon?). Therefore, the cooler air would be drawn in close to the ground as hot air was pulled out of the house at the top. Another natural cooling device was the operable transom. Placed above interior doors, transoms allowed air to flow through the house while still providing occupants with privacy. We can employ these same techniques today to keep our homes naturally cool.

The type of window you choose can also help. Double-hung windows were invented for a reason. They can be opened both from the bottom and the top, which provides flexibility in promoting air movement. First-floor windows could be opened from the bottom, while second-floor windows could be opened from the top, again promoting good natural convection currents. Even in a single room, opening each sash a few inches can help pull cooler air in at the bottom of the window while allowing warmer air to be vented at the top. The taller the window, the better this works.

NATURAL VENTILATION

Double-hung windows are designed to admit cooler air at the bottom and exhaust warmer air at the top.

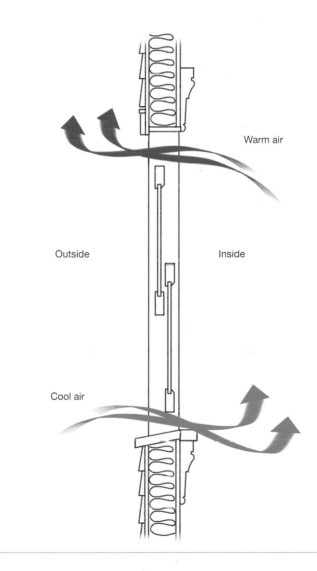

Warm air

Outside

Inside

Cool air

DESIGNING WITH SUNLIGHT

Natural light has a potent influence on our emotional response to any home. When we walk into a bright house we naturally feel good, even if we can't put our finger on the reason. If a home is dark, we feel vaguely troubled, again perhaps without knowing exactly why. Remodeling provides us with the perfect opportunity to find new ways of bringing light into the place where we spend the vast majority of our time.

Even interior rooms without windows can be brightened up with sunlight by the use of skylights. When proximity to the roof is a problem, tubular skylights can bring sunlight into rooms where traditional skylights would be impractical.

▲▲ **Designing with light: The dining room of this green remodel in Newton, Massachusetts, is bathed in a warm glow thanks to the architect's decision to open up a wall, admitting daylight that pours in from a large Palladian window above the stairs.**

◄ **This interior hallway is illuminated by a solar tube, a round metal sleeve with a highly reflective interior reaching from a small clear dome on the roof to an interior space that wouldn't otherwise receive any daylight.**

SELECTIVE SHADING

Regardless of what kind of windows you have in your remodel, it is important to think about which direction they face and the amount of sunlight that enters through them. Particularly on the south side of a house, you can employ some passive solar strategies to take advantage of free heating in the winter.

At the same time, you don't want too much sunlight heating up the house in summer when you're trying to keep cool. One answer is selective exterior shading. The sun is higher in the sky in summer than it is in winter. Understanding this makes it possible to create a shading device that allows direct sunlight to pour in during the winter months when the sun is low in the sky, but shades the window from the summer sun.

Shade structures can take a variety of forms, and the choice will have a lot to do with the style of your own home. Traditional awnings were invented for this very purpose and still can be a great solution. But architectural devices such as correctly sized roof overhangs or canopies will also do the trick.

Some remodeling projects lend themselves more readily to passive solar than others, simply because the existing house, and its surroundings, may make it difficult to optimize the home's solar orientation. But for many homes this can be an invaluable strategy to have in the remodeler's bag of tricks.

The sun is higher in the sky in summer than it is in winter, so a correctly sized roof overhang or other shading device can shade the interior from unwanted solar gain in the summer and admit direct sunlight in the winter.

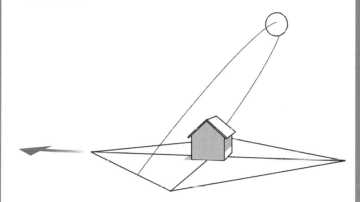

PATH OF THE SUMMER SUN
Sunlight falling on the south side of a house at noon in mid July. The size of the roof overhang is calculated to shade the south-facing windows from the summer sun, keeping the house from overheating.

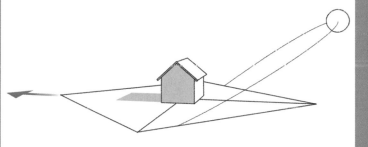

PATH OF THE WINTER SUN
The same house at noon in late November, when the lower angle of the sun allows full sunlight to enter, providing light and warmth.

Extended rafter tails with wood slats shade south-facing windows of a house in Salem, Oregon, from the summer sun without casting dark shadows. In winter, the sun's rays, coming from a lower angle in the sky, flood the house with light and provide passive solar heating.

Light has different qualities at each point on the compass, so when you're remodeling you need to consider each side of the house accordingly. From the north we get soft, even illumination throughout the day but no direct sunlight. This is why artists have always favored studios with north light. But we get no solar gain from it, so in colder climates it is best to avoid large expanses of glass on the north side or we risk losing too much heat.

Eastern light is strongest in the morning, making the east side an attractive spot for kitchens and breakfast rooms. The solar gain from eastern light is not a problem in the warmer months because by the hottest part of the day the sun has traveled to the other side of the house.

Western light is particularly difficult to control. As the sun moves toward the horizon, its intense late-afternoon rays pour it on. We get harsh shadows all year and overheating in the summer. For that reason, this can be a good place to put the garage and other utility areas, shielding the home's interior from harsh sunlight.

A southern exposure, however, offers multiple benefits. As the sun moves across the sky, the south side of a house remains in full sun all day. (Unless you live in the southern hemisphere, in which case, it's the reverse.) This is where shading devices such as roof overhangs, awnings, or pergolas enable us to take advantage of passive solar gain.

By placing materials such as stone, brick, tile, or concrete in areas that receive southern sunlight, we create thermal mass, which absorbs the sun's heat during the day and releases it slowly during the night, reducing the demands on heating equipment. Installing a double layer of drywall on walls that receive direct sunlight is another, and less expensive, way of creating thermal mass.

Sustainability is not something that can be applied to a house like a coat of paint. It is the result of the creative integration of the three fundamentals of green remodeling in ways that amplify and reinforce one another. Scattered throughout the pages of this book you can see examples of how homeowners and designers around the country have put all the green design strategies discussed in this chapter, and more, to practical use, creating homes in a wide variety of styles that are green by design.

DESIGNING WITH SUNLIGHT

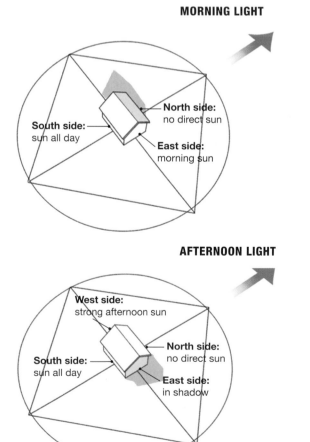

MORNING LIGHT

South side: sun all day

North side: no direct sun

East side: morning sun

AFTERNOON LIGHT

West side: strong afternoon sun

South side: sun all day

North side: no direct sun

East side: in shadow

Thermal mass, provided by flooring materials such as stone, tile, and concrete or by walls with a double layer of drywall, absorbs the sun's heat during the day and releases it slowly into the home's interior after the sun has gone down.

AN UPSIDE-DOWN HOUSE IN TEXAS

BEFORE

AFTER

When the owners first saw the house, they were undeterred by the dark, ugly kitchen. Using a sophisticated palette of sustainable materials, their vision transformed the space into a bright, lively hub for all the activities of a growing family.

It is quite possible that only a husband and wife who are both architects could have seen the potential hiding in the dark, dysfunctional, upside-down house with tired 1980s decor. The unusual arrangement of rooms—kitchen, living/dining room, and master bedroom on the second floor and kids' bedrooms and family room on the ground floor—posed a particular challenge for Al and Sharon, young parents who didn't want to feel isolated from their three little boys. The floors were connected by a cramped, enclosed stair, and the entry vestibule could only be described as claustrophobic.

"The rituals of our lives revolved so much around not separating activities," Al said. "When I'm home working, I don't want to be completely isolated from what's going on in the house. We needed to reconfigure the way the house worked so that it would make sense for the way we live."

The space needed to facilitate diverse activities. In the morning, that means getting breakfast for three kids, packing lunch, and making snacks. During the day, it's keeping an eye on the boys, trying to get some work done, and occasionally needing to run a load of laundry in the midst of it all. And in the evening, it's time for homework, cooking dinner, and having some family time. The space needed to be flexible and open, with essential functions within easy reach.

Ceiling panels of natural, renewable, and sound-absorbing cork not only improve the space's acoustical properties but also blend beautifully with the home's earth-toned palette.

PROJECT AT A GLANCE

Originally built: 1982

Original size: 1,100 sq. ft.

Size after remodel: 1,100 sq. ft.

Architect: McKinney-York Architects

Location: Austin, Texas

FIRST FLOOR (BEFORE)

FIRST FLOOR (AFTER)

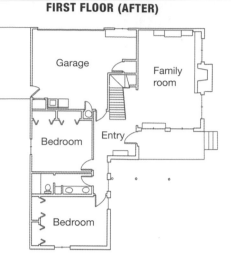

SECOND FLOOR (BEFORE)

SECOND FLOOR (AFTER)

OPENING UP THE PLAN

To open up and visually expand the space, walls separating the foyer from the family room and hallway were removed. A new open stair was turned around so that it draws guests up from the expanded entry to the living level on the second floor.

The kitchen in the old plan was a dead end. In the reconfigured space, circulation rings a vertical service core with laundry machines, a pantry, and HVAC equipment. A wall was removed to open up a tiny room off the kitchen, turning it into an office that doubles as a place for the kids to do homework. "In the evening, we can be cooking while they're on the computer or drawing and they don't feel isolated from us," said Al.

▲ Reconfiguring traffic flow can conserve resources by adding useful space without increasing the size of a home. Opening up the entry hall and reorienting the stair improved circulation in this Texas home and provided a sense of spaciousness in place of the cramped original foyer. Daylight from the second floor now helps illuminate the lower level.

◄ The home office was opened up to the kitchen and fitted out with formaldehyde-free MDF cabinetry. On the floor, eco-friendly carpet tiles are made with renewable and recycled content. (The manufacturer will take back old carpet squares and recycle them into new product.)

LOW-MAINTENANCE MATERIALS

Sustainable materials and energy efficiency were high priorities. Much of the interior is paneled in formaldehyde-free, exterior-grade medium-density fiberboard (MDF). It is highly durable and moisture resistant and forgiving of small handprints.

New, thermally broken double-pane aluminum windows were installed, and the walls were well insulated to provide a tight, well-sealed thermal envelope. The old energy-hungry furnace was replaced with a high-efficiency unit that could be vented through the side wall, eliminating the need for a chimney. New ductwork was tested for leaks and sealed to optimize efficiency. The 10-SEER (seasonal energy efficiency rating) air conditioners were replaced with 14-SEER

▲◄► On the upper level, circulation was reorganized around a central core that houses mechanical equipment, laundry machines, and a pantry. Opening up the connections between rooms allows for more informal family interaction and also provides diners with a view of the treetops.

▼◄ In the kitchen, a large corner window floods the space with natural light while visually expanding the space.

▼► A low partition between the kitchen and dining area allows daylight to illuminate both spaces. The shallow storage unit tucked into the divider provides child-height access to things like napkins and salt-and-pepper shakers.

units, and air cleaners with 5-in. pleated media filters were added to help keep pollutants out.

After solving the functional problems, the other priority was aesthetics. The home's 1980-vintage interior hadn't aged well. And for a couple of architects, as Sharon said, "living with something not beautiful is hard."

The interior materials were chosen for low emissions, durability, and economy. Sheathed in dark-stained MDF, the vertical core, containing the stair, a pantry, and laundry center, became a central organizing feature of the house. The open stair provides a strong visual and acoustical connection between the two floors.

The boomerang-shaped kitchen island contains a convenient recycling center and serves as the command center for this busy household. A large corner soffit defines the work area and integrates efficient lighting into a luminous ceiling that joins directly to the insulated glass corner windows.

Al and Sharon knew that one drawback of an open-plan space with hard surfaces might be excessive noise. To absorb some of the sound waves, they decided to finish the living room's ceiling in cork. It's a rapidly renewable, all-natural material, and the natural color harmonizes with the home's warm color palette.

* Low-maintenance materials include MDF paneling and kitchen cabinets, which don't require painting.

* Low-emitting materials are used, including:
  • Natural cork
  • Formaldehyde-free MDF
  • Zero-VOC paint

* The recyclable commercial carpet tiles are from InterfaceFLOR™. There is only 3% waste compared with 25% waste for carpet in rolls, and it's easy to replace one tile if stained, so the floor has a long life expectancy. This environmentally friendly material meets the carpet and rug industry's highest environmental standard, the Carpet and Rug Institute's (CRI) Green Label Plus.

* The recycling center has a trash compactor for aluminum cans, plastics, etc., and a dedicated drawer with extra-heavy-duty glides to collect newspapers.

* The luminous ceiling has high-efficiency T-5 fluorescent bulbs.

* Paper shades hang over compact fluorescent bulbs.

* The corner window brings in ample natural light so electric lights are not needed during the day.

BUTTONING UP:
CREATING A TIGHT THERMAL ENVELOPE

In chapter 2 we looked at a number of strategies for making houses more energy efficient, the first fundamental of green remodeling. Here, we'll focus more closely on ways to reduce a home's demand for heating and cooling, which I referred to as strategy 1.

This category includes various ways of optimizing the thermal properties of the building envelope. In the simplest terms, the building envelope is everything that stands between you and the great outdoors. The building envelope keeps out things we don't want inside the house, both climate related and physical. Climate-related things include rain, snow, wind, and excessive cold and heat, while the more physical things can be small and inanimate (airborne allergens and contaminants like dust, pollen, mold spores, and soot) or larger and more animated (insects, birds, wild animals, and other unwelcome guests—some with as few as two legs).

WHILE YOU'RE AT IT...

Some remodeling projects—putting on an addition, replacing windows, or other renovations that involve substantial changes to the home's exterior—inherently involve decisions about how to keep the cold out and the heat in. But even projects with little or no impact on the building envelope—interior upgrades like kitchen or bath remodels or the reconfiguring of interior space—might encourage you to think about other parts of your home.

Any green remodeling project, no matter how limited in scope, can be seen as an opportunity to think about what else might be done to make the rest of the house greener. Improvements such as air sealing, weatherstripping, and attic insulation are relatively simple and inexpensive but can make a big difference in the home's overall comfort and energy efficiency. Here are a few suggestions for simple green upgrades for the rest of the house when you're remodeling:

- ☼ Check windows and doors for air infiltration, and add weatherstripping and door sweeps where needed.

- ☼ Upgrade attic insulation: Many attics have too little insulation or gaps in the insulation that exacerbate heat loss. This is easy to correct while work is being done elsewhere in the house.

- ☼ Replace old carpeting: Wall-to-wall carpeting is a magnet for all sorts of dirt, pollutants, and allergens. Now could be a good time to replace it with new carpet with a tighter weave (easier to keep clean) or, better still, a hard surface that can be damp-mopped such as tile, cork, wood, or linoleum.

- ☼ Have your heating and air-conditioning equipment tuned up and replace furnace filters.

BUILDING SCIENCE: THREE TYPES OF HEAT TRANSFER

To better understand the various ways the building envelope contributes to the home's thermal performance, it is helpful to know how heat is transferred from one place to another. There are three types of heat transfer: conduction, convection, and radiant.

Conduction is the transfer of heat between adjoining substances or materials. If you hold a bowl of ice cream in your hand, the bowl, which is a poor insulator, conducts heat from your body to the ice cream, with the result that the ice cream begins to melt and you begin to feel colder. The same thing happens in the winter when you're building a snowman or making snowballs—especially if you're not wearing gloves. Just as a good pair of gloves and a warm coat slow the loss of body heat when you're playing in the snow, insulation prevents conductive heat transfer between the air inside your house and the air outside your house, which are both in contact with the wall that separates them. A well-insulated wall creates a thermal break between the cold outside air and the warmer air inside your house. Insulation reduces the wall's thermal conductivity, slowing conductive heat loss.

Convection is the transfer of heat through air movement. Gaps that allow air to pass through the home's thermal envelope cause heat loss by convection. The more effective insulation is at preventing the flow of air, the better it performs. Warm air escaping through gaps under doors or up the chimney are two examples of convective heat loss.

Radiant transfer is the movement of heat between things that are not in physical contact. You feel the sun's heat because of radiant transfer. You feel cold when standing or sitting near a window with uninsulated glass on a winter day because your body is losing heat to the glass via radiant transfer. And the reverse is true when you stand near an old-fashioned cast-iron radiator.

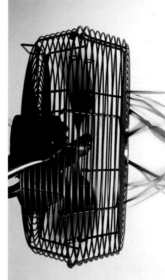

▲◄ **Conduction:** When you hold something cold, like a snowball, heat from your warm body is transferred to the colder object. As the snowball begins to melt, you start to feel colder. The insulation provided by a pair of gloves, like the insulation in your walls, would slow the conductive heat loss and you'd feel more comfortable.

◄ That's why they're called radiators: **Radiation** is the mode of heat movement that transfers the warmth of a cast-iron radiator to cooler objects not in physical contact with it, like your body and everything else in the room.

▲ **Convection:** On a hot summer day, the breeze from an electric fan makes you feel cooler because some of the heat your body radiates is whisked away by currents of moving air. But in winter, when you want your house to stay warm, sealing air leaks will prevent convective heat loss.

SEALING AIR LEAKS

The average house leaks air like a sieve, which is responsible for losing a great deal of heat through convective transfer. Sealing air leaks is the simplest, most cost-effective way to reduce heat loss. It saves you money and eliminates drafts, making your house more comfortable.

The most critical air leaks in most homes are in the attic and the basement. When your heating system warms the air inside your house, the warm air, because it is more buoyant than cold air, naturally rises. As your expensively heated air rises, finding its way through numerous small gaps into the attic, cold air is pulled in through leaks in the basement, around windows and doors, and elsewhere. This creates a chimney effect that continuously sucks the heat out of your house.

Can a house be too airtight?

The number of air changes per hour (ACH) is the standard measure of how tight or leaky a house is. The average new home typically has an ACH of around 1.75. That means all the air in the house is changed 1.75 times per hour, or about 40 times per day. In poorly sealed older homes, air leakage can be 2.5 ACH, or even higher. That's 60 or more complete air changes per day. All the air that leaks out of the house carries heat with it. Every air change means more fresh air that must be heated or cooled.

To achieve maximum energy efficiency, we want to create a tight thermal envelope with as close to zero air changes per hour as possible. And with the right insulation and careful attention to air sealing, we can come pretty close to zero. The only problem is that we need fresh air. In a house with no air exchange, we wouldn't feel very well. There would be less oxygen in the air.

COMMON SOURCES OF AIR LEAKS

Seal the leaks in the attic with caulk and expanding foam before adding insulation. You may have to remove some of the existing insulation to find all the leaks. Next, seal air leaks around doors and windows with caulk or weatherstripping. Doing a thorough job will make a big difference in your comfort and your energy bills.

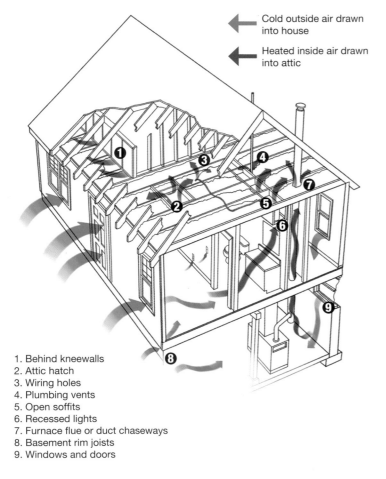

Cold outside air drawn into house

Heated inside air drawn into attic

1. Behind kneewalls
2. Attic hatch
3. Wiring holes
4. Plumbing vents
5. Open soffits
6. Recessed lights
7. Furnace flue or duct chaseways
8. Basement rim joists
9. Windows and doors

Adapted from www.energystar.gov

Fumes from cooking, as well as other airborne pollutants, would build up and get recirculated throughout the house, creating unhealthy air quality.

Mechanical ventilation What, then, is the right balance between energy efficiency and health? A frequently repeated mantra in green building circles is "build tight and ventilate right." The ideal rate of air exchange to prevent unwanted heat loss but preserve good indoor air quality is about 0.33 ACH—one-third of the air exchanged per hour, or eight complete air changes per day. Achieving that controlled rate of exchange requires mechanical ventilation. A small exhaust fan and one window left slightly ajar could do the trick, but the fan would constantly be pulling heat out of the house along with stale air.

The best way to provide controlled ventilation in a tightly sealed home is with an air-to-air heat exchanger, commonly known as an energy-recovery ventilator (ERV), or a heat-recovery ventilator (HRV). Typically installed in the attic or basement and connected to the home's ductwork, these devices capture thermal energy from the stale exhaust air and use it to precondition the fresh air entering the house. In the heating season, the warmth from the exhaust air preheats the cold fresh air being brought in from outside. And in cooling season, the conditioned exhaust air cools and dehumidifies the warmer outdoor air.

The difference between ERVs and HRVs has to do with moisture. ERVs also preserve the humidity levels inside the house, keeping the air from getting overly dry in winter or too humid in summer. In dry climates, where there is minimal change in humidity levels from summer to winter, an HRV, which doesn't have the moisture exchange feature found in ERVs, can be used.

HRVs and ERVs generally have an efficiency rating of about 70%. This means that while they are replacing all the air in the house with fresh air, there is only a 30% heat loss. That might sound like a lot of heat going out the door, but compared with the amount of heat lost in a home leaking at the rate of 2.5 ACH, it is miniscule.

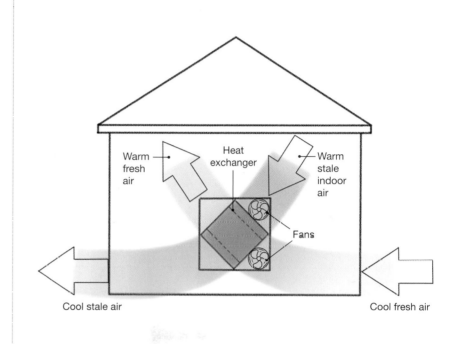

ENERGY-RECOVERY VENTILATOR

Warm fresh air

Heat exchanger

Warm stale indoor air

Fans

Cool stale air

Cool fresh air

Improvements to the building envelope make a big difference in energy efficiency and should be a high priority for any green remodeling project.

THE BUILDING ENVELOPE

The building envelope is made up of the home's structural elements: foundation walls, concrete slabs, and the aboveground structure—studs, rafters, sheathing, roofing, siding, flashing and other waterproofing materials, as well as the things that keep the heat in (or out, depending on the season) like insulation, windows, and doors.

I like to think about houses from the ground up. Chapter 7 will delve more deeply into different types of foundations and their relative merits, but a discussion of a home's thermal envelope wouldn't be complete without considering how the foundation contributes to the home's energy performance. Most foundations do not make any positive contribution to the thermal envelope—worse, they more often have a negative effect. But they don't have to.

The foundation

Concrete is a poor insulator. No, let me restate that: Concrete has no insulating properties whatsoever. (Concrete's R-value of 0.08 per inch is close enough to zero to be considered essentially nil.) But it does have other thermal properties that can be used to our advantage. What it has is thermal mass. That means it can absorb and hold heat. Like a chameleon taking on the color of its surroundings, concrete will acclimate to the temperature of whatever it is in contact with. Except for in the most extreme climate zones, the temperature of the earth a few feet below the surface is fairly constant at about 50°F or so, summer and winter. So concrete in direct contact with the surrounding earth will also be about 50°F. The slab—the concrete floor of the basement—will also be the same temperature.

But how much difference can this make to a home's energy efficiency? Most people understand that heat rises. Or they think they do. But that is not strictly the case. Hot *air* rises. This is because warm air is more buoyant than cool air. But heat itself moves from warmer areas to

Heat radiates from warmer to colder objects. The cold concrete of uninsulated foundations draws heat out of the house.

AIR LEAKS CAUSE EXCESSIVE DRYNESS

Air leaks rob your home of moisture, which is the reason houses feel dry in the winter. All that warm air leaking out of the house carries humidity with it, leaving the air inside the house dry and uncomfortable. In tightly sealed homes, much less moisture is lost and the air feels more comfortable.

As shown below, it would take an entire year for half of a cup of water to diffuse through a 100-sq.-ft. wall with no vapor barrier. But if that wall contains small air leaks totaling just 1 sq. in., 100 cups of water can pass through by convection in the same amount of time.

IMPORTANCE OF AIR SEALING FOR HUMIDITY CONTROL

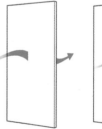

DIFFUSION
100 sq. ft. of wall = ½ cup of water per year

AIR LEAKAGE
1-sq.-in. hole = 100 cups per year

INSULATING A BASEMENT

In most cases, it isn't practical to expose the outside of the foundation of an existing house. But if your renovation includes an addition, consider insulating the foundation from the outside. The best material to do this with is rigid foam, which comes in sheets of varying thickness. One inch is good; two is better. Insulating under the slab is also recommended. If you can't do both, I recommend insulating the slab. It's always possible to insulate the basement walls from the inside later on, but there's not much you can do about the floor once the concrete is poured. Especially if the basement will be used for living space, you don't want the floor to be cold.

Insulating basement walls and slabs can improve indoor air quality, too, because it prevents unwanted moisture. Condensation forms on surfaces that are colder than the dew point of the surrounding air. You see this every time you sip a glass of iced tea on a warm day. This can cause cold concrete surfaces to become damp, which can encourage the growth of mold. So insulating your basement properly not only improves the home's thermal performance but also can help ensure good indoor air quality. Yet another benefit of insulating concrete from the outside is that it puts thermal mass on the inside of the home's thermal envelope where it can do the most good. Insulated concrete actually stores heat rather than drawing it out of the house.

If you can't insulate the outside of the foundation, there are still significant improvements to be achieved by insulating from the inside. You won't get the benefit of the concrete's thermal mass, but it will improve your home's comfort and energy efficiency.

colder areas. Without any insulating barrier to slow it down, some of the heat in your house is absorbed by the concrete walls and floor of your basement. This makes the foundation a heat sink—a kind of negative radiator.

Why, then, doesn't the concrete become warm? It would, in fact, if there were something to keep the heat absorbed by the concrete from being conducted to the outside. Most basements, if they are insulated at all, are insulated from the inside. If done properly, this will keep most of the heat from escaping, or at least slow it down. This is not a bad solution, but there are better ones.

If concrete is insulated from the outside, it gradually absorbs heat and holds it. This can be a great energy saver because once the concrete absorbs heat, the exterior insulation slows the conductive transfer from the concrete to the earth, and some of that heat can then radiate back into your house.

The wall assembly

When thinking about the thermal envelope of a house, it is helpful to look at the walls as a system. The frame, usually

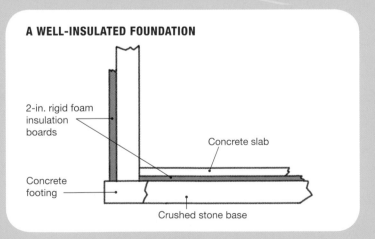

A WELL-INSULATED FOUNDATION

2-in. rigid foam insulation boards

Concrete slab

Concrete footing

Crushed stone base

In most remodels, the foundation can't be insulated from the outside. Insulating the inside of a basement foundation with rigid expanded polystyrene sheets is an affordable alternative that reduces heat loss. For fire safety, the insulation board should be covered by drywall.

made of 2x4s or sometimes 2x6s, is covered on the outside with rigid sheathing—either plywood or oriented strand board (OSB). Ideally, the sheathing is covered with house wrap, a waterproof material that is vapor permeable in one direction. House wrap protects the wall assembly from water that might find its way through the siding (some always does) but allows any moisture that is in the walls to escape to the outside. It also serves as an air barrier to help reduce air infiltration and convective heat loss.

The outside of the wall is finished with siding, whether clapboard, shingle, brick, stone, or a number of other possibilities. All types of siding are designed to shed water, but no siding can be relied on to be absolutely, infallibly, 100% weather-proof. House wrap is your second line of defense.

House wraps are made of material designed to keep water out while allowing moisture in the wall cavity to escape.

Insulation choices The inside of the wall is generally finished with drywall and the cavity is filled with insulation to slow the transfer of heat from one side of the wall to the other. But what kind of insulation is best? Before going into detail about the different types of insulation that are available, I need to tell you a little bad news about insulation in general. Whatever type of insulation you choose, it does not extend uniformly across the entire wall. Every 16 in. it is interrupted by a stud. And wood is not as good an insulator as whatever you put between the studs. So when you install R-19 batts, you are not getting an R-19 wall. Even if the insulation is installed perfectly, a 2x6 wall with R-19 batts will give you an insulation value of about R-17.

But, and this is a big but, when you factor in the numerous small gaps that are common with less than perfectly installed insulation, convective heat loss can reduce the wall's total R-value to as little as half of the insulation's rating.

To repeat what I wrote in chapter 2, unless the insulation is installed perfectly (which in the real world is rare), there can be numerous small gaps where two pieces of insulation meet, at the top of the wall if a piece is cut just a little short, where the insulation gets stuffed behind a pipe or an electrical outlet, or where it meets a window or door frame. All these little gaps, if added together, can be responsible for as much heat loss as leaving a window open. To be effective, insulating with fiberglass batts must be accompanied with careful and thorough air sealing.

A better way to insulate is to use either blown-in cellulose or sprayed foam, both of which provide greater resistance to air leakage. Both types completely fill every crevasse of the wall cavity, virtually eliminating the possibility of gaps. So the wall assembly will perform much closer

▲◄ Fiberglass batts must be installed with care to avoid leaving small gaps that reduce the wall's resistance to heat flow.

◄ One of the great advantages of cellulose insulation is that it can be blown into existing wall cavities with minimal disruption.

▲ Because of sprayed foam insulation's superior air-sealing properties, 1 in. of it is as effective as 6 in. of fiberglass.

COMPARATIVE R-VALUES FOR DIFFERENT TYPES OF INSULATION

MATERIAL	R-VALUE PER INCH	R-VALUE 2X4 WALLS*	R-VALUE PER 2x6 WALLS
Framing lumber	1.25	4.4	6.9
Fiberglass batts	3.5	12.3	19.3
Cotton batts (recycled denim)	3.7	13.0	20.4
Blown-in cellulose	3.7	13.0	20.4
Low-density sprayed foam	4.2	14.7	23
Rigid foam high-R boards	5.5	19.3	30.3
High-density sprayed foam	6.25	21.9	34.4

*Does not account for studs, windows, or other wall penetrations. Total wall assembly R-values will be lower.

to the material's rated R-value. Cellulose, made from recycled newspaper which makes it espe-cially green, has an insulating value of about R-3.7 per inch, similar to fiberglass. R-value is not the whole story, though. While cellulose, which is more expensive than fiberglass, has roughly the same R-value per inch, its ability to prevent air infiltration provides significantly better thermal performance.

Sprayed foam, depending on the type, ranges from R-3.7 to more than R-6 per inch. Low-density, open-cell foam is at the lower end of that spectrum, while high-density closed-cell foam is at the upper end. Sprayed foam is more expensive than either fiberglass batts or cellulose, but its superior performance can make the initial cost a worthwhile investment. Because of its superior air-sealing characteristics, 1 in. of sprayed foam will outperform 6 in. of fiberglass.

Because high-density foam is significantly more expensive than low-density foam, it is some-times used as part of a hybrid system composed of 2 in. of high-density foam applied to the interior of the sheathing, with the remainder of the cavity filled with fiberglass, cellulose, or low-density foam.

Cellulose insulation, shown in this attic retrofit, is made from recycled newspapers. Its excellent insulating properties and low embod-ied energy make it a very green choice.

LESS WOOD = MORE INSULATION

Considering wood's low resistance to conductive heat transfer, what if we were to use less of it? A great way to improve the thermal envelope is to employ advanced framing techniques that reduce the amount of wood used to frame the house. This conserves lumber, saves money, and allows for more insulation. Wood has a lower R-value than the insulation between the studs. In homes framed with studs 16 in. on center, about 15% of the wall area is solid wood. Increasing that spacing to 24 in. on center allows room for about 10% more insulation. Chapter 7 examines advanced framing techniques in more detail. But for now, just keep in mind that less wood equals more insulation.

Advanced framing techniques re-duce the amount of lumber used for framing, saving money, conserving timber resources, and allowing more room for insulation.

TYPES OF INSULATION

	HOW INSTALLED	PROS	CONS	COMMENTS	R-VALUE PER INCH*	COST
Fiberglass batts	Fitted between studs and joists	Lowest cost; easy to install, even for do-it-yourselfers	Not an air barrier; requires careful installation and thorough air sealing; many brands contain formaldehyde; high embodied energy	Look for formaldehyde-free fiberglass; rock wool batts are similar but have higher density	3.0 to 4.0	Low
Cotton batts	Fitted between studs and joists	Relatively easy to install; has higher density, so provides some protection from air infiltration; nontoxic; 80% postindustrial recycled content	More expensive than fiberglass batts	Not available in all areas	3.0 to 3.7	Moderate
Blown-in cellulose	Blown into wall cavities, floors, and ceilings	Easily fills most gaps; provides very good protection from air infiltration; useful for retrofits of existing walls; 80% postconsumer recycled content; low embodied energy; nontoxic	Highly chemically sensitive individuals may experience allergic reactions from printer's ink in recycled newspapers	Requires specialized equipment to install; not for do-it-yourselfers	3.6 to 4.0	Moderate
Blown-in fiberglass	Blown into wall cavities, floors, and ceilings	Easily fills most gaps; provides very good protection from air infiltration; useful for retrofits of existing walls	Inhaling fibers poses health concerns	Requires specialized equipment to install; not for do-it-yourselfers		
Sprayed foam	Sprayed in place	Fills virtually all gaps; provides excellent protection from air infiltration	Relatively high embodied energy but more than offset by resulting energy savings	Requires specialized equipment to install; not for do-it-yourselfers	3.6 to 4.0	Moderate
Open-cell (low-density)					3.6 to 3.8	High
Closed-cell (high-density)					5.8 to 6.8	Highest
Rigid foam		Relatively easy to install; high R-values; excellent air barrier; can be used on walls, roofs, and foundations	Many brands use ozone-depleting blowing agents in manufacturing	Look for foams that do not use hydrochlorofluorocarbons (HCFCs) or cholorfluorocarbons (CFCs)	3.6 to 6.8	Moderate

*Does not account for studs, windows, or other wall penetrations. Total wall assembly R-values will be lower.

Wood's low resistance to heat loss creates a condition known as thermal bridging, which means that heat and cold are transferred more easily through wood framing members—studs and rafters—than through the insulation. You can observe this in the winter when there is a light dusting of snow on roofs. Heat escaping into the attic from below is conducted to the roofing through the rafters, making the snow melt faster there than on the rest of the roof that is better insulated, creating a striped pattern that shows exactly where the rafters are located.

There are a few solutions to thermal bridging. In homes with unfinished attics, sprayed foam can be applied not only between the rafters but also over them. Or, thermal bridging can be dealt with from the outside. Spaceloft® Insul-Cap™, a new product containing aerogel, a space-age material that may be the world's most efficient insulation, clocking in at an amazing R-15 per inch, can be attached to the outside of the studs prior to installing the sheathing. The ¼-in.-thick strips are 1½ in. wide, exactly the size of a stud, and have an insulation value of about R-4.

Yet another solution for a high-performance building envelope is to add insulation to the outside using rigid foam high-R board. Especially when used in conjunction with some other type of insulation within the wall cavity, this can create a thermal envelope that is highly resistant to heat loss.

Windows Glass, like concrete, has no insulation value on its own, other than stopping the wind from blowing through the house. In windows with so-called insulated glass, it is the air space between the panes that provides some insulation value. Some gases are more resistant to heat transfer than air. Windows made with argon or krypton gas between the panes do a better job of slowing heat transfer.

Applying various metallic coatings to the glass can reduce radiant heat transfer by changing the emissivity of the glass. Emissivity is a measure of how easily heat is radiated to or from

▲◄ Spraying foam insulation over the exposed rafters is one way to eliminate thermal bridging.

▲▲ Insul-Cap, made from space-age aerogel material, adds R-4 of insulation value with just a ¼-in.-thick strip. Here it is being used to provide a thermal break between a stud and the wall sheathing to prevent thermal bridging.

▲ One inch of rigid foam insulation is applied to the exterior walls of a new addition; the seams will be taped to provide a continuous, airtight thermal barrier. This extra layer of insulation is rated at R-5.5, but because thermal bridging is eliminated, the effective R-value of the complete wall assembly is considerably higher.

Large expanses of glass make a room feel light and airy, but most windows have very low resistance to heat loss.

a given material. Glass with such metallic coatings is known as low-E glass. Low-E glass slows the radiant loss of heat through the window in winter as well as reducing unwanted solar gain in summer.

A well-made window resists all three kinds of heat transfer. The air or other gas sealed between the panes of insulated glass slows **conductive** heat loss, as does a well-insulated frame made of materials that don't conduct heat easily. (Fiberglass window frames are especially resistant to conducting heat. Aluminum conducts heat very well, so windows with aluminum frames require a thermal break, made of a low-conducting material, between the interior and exterior surfaces.) Tight construction prevents air leakage, reducing **convective** heat loss. And low-E coatings, designed to reflect light of various wavelengths, slow **radiant** heat loss.

Still, even the best windows made by the major manufacturers have an insulating value of only about R-3. We love having lots of big windows because daylight and views outside make us feel good and because lots of daylight means you don't have to turn on the lights during the day, which saves energy. But even top-of-the-line windows have poor R-values compared with the rest of the building envelope.

Eliminating all of your windows would make your house really energy efficient. But, for obvious reasons, no one would do that. Making the rest of the home's thermal envelope as tight and well insulated as possible is a reasonable compromise between energy efficiency and a pleasant living space full of daylight. But innovations in glazing technology now make much more efficient windows possible.

Several manufacturers, most notably a company called Serious Materials, now offer windows made with Southwall Technology's ultra-efficient Heat Mirror® glass. Originally developed at MIT, Heat Mirror glass employs a clear polyester film suspended in the air space between the two panes of insulating glass. Options include several types of low-E coatings and gas-filled spaces. Various climate-specific combinations of low-E coatings on the film and on the glass and krypton gas in one or more of the spaces can produce windows with insulating values as high as R-11 (U-value of 0.09).

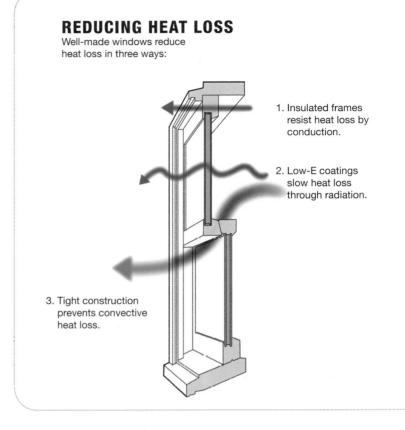

REDUCING HEAT LOSS
Well-made windows reduce heat loss in three ways:

1. Insulated frames resist heat loss by conduction.

2. Low-E coatings slow heat loss through radiation.

3. Tight construction prevents convective heat loss.

HOW TO READ THE NATIONAL FENESTRATION RATING COUNCIL (NFRC) LABEL

U-FACTOR: Resistance to heat loss; lower numbers represent better thermal performance.

VISIBLE TRANSMITTANCE: Amount of visible light admitted; higher numbers represent more light.

CONDENSATION RESISTANCE: Better windows are more resistant to condensation; higher CR numbers represent lower condensation.

SOLAR HEAT GAIN COEFFICIENT: Resistance to solar gain; windows with lower numbers admit less of the sun's heat.

AIR LEAKAGE: Tightly built windows have lower AL numbers.

NFRC — National Fenestration Rating Council® CERTIFIED	World's Best Window Co.
	Millennium 2000+
	Vinyl-Clad Wood Frame
	Double Glazing • Argon Fill • Low E
	Product Type: **Vertical Slider**

ENERGY PERFORMANCE RATINGS	
U-Factor (U.S./I-P)	Solar Heat Gain Coefficient
0.35	**0.32**

ADDITIONAL PERFORMANCE RATINGS	
Visible Transmittance	Air Leakage (U.S./I-P)
0.51	**0.2**
Condensation Resistance	
51	—

Manufacturer stipulates that these ratings conform to applicable NFRC procedures for determining whole product performance. NFRC ratings are determined for a fixed set of environmental conditions and a specific product size. NFRC does not recommend any product and does not warrant the suitability of any product for any specific use. Consult manufacturer's literature for other product performance information.
www.nfrc.org

DOES IT PAY TO REPLACE YOUR WINDOWS?

Until recently, the conventional wisdom about window replacements was that the payback was too long to make it worthwhile. But that advice was always predicated on upgrading to windows with ordinary low-E insulating glass, which typically have insulating values of around R-2.8 to R-3. But when you run the same calculation for what I call super windows, you get a very different answer. My definition of a super window is one that performs at R-5 or higher. One of the pioneers in the field, Serious Materials, makes residential windows that range all the way up to R-11.

If you are replacing typical low- to mid-performing windows (R-1 to R-2.5), such as are found in most homes, with R-5 windows, you can expect a 25% to 40% reduction in energy costs. Depending on the cost of energy where you live, the windows will have a straight-line payback period of 3 to 10 years.

The payback looks much more attractive if you are financing your replacement windows. If you spend $8,000 to replace the windows in your house with R-5 units, your energy bills should go down by as much as $200 per month. Yet, if you are paying for those windows with a 20-year amortizing loan at 6.5%, your monthly payment will be just under $60.

This does not take into account the up-front savings on new HVAC equipment and ductwork, which will be smaller due to the home's reduced heating and cooling loads. If your remodel includes new heating and cooling systems, upgrading to super windows may not add much to your budget at all. Surprisingly, super windows are competitively priced compared with standard windows of similar construction.

SUPER WINDOWS

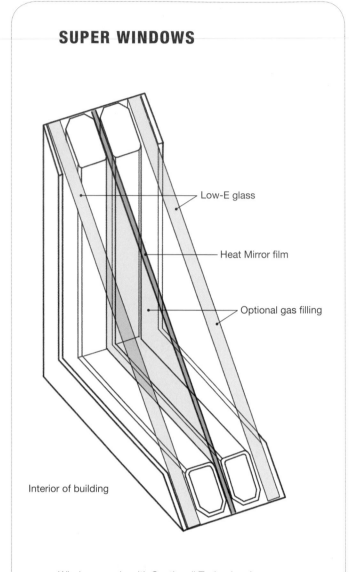

Low-E glass

Heat Mirror film

Optional gas filling

Interior of building

Windows made with Southwall Technology's Heat Mirror glass, used by Serious Materials and other manufacturers, provide insulation values from R-5 to as much as R-11.

Radiant barriers In warm climates where air-conditioning is used more than heating, solar gain counts for a large part of the cooling load. Windows with a high solar heat gain coefficient can reduce the amount of unwanted solar heating, but windows aren't the only part of the building envelope that can deflect excess solar gain from the home.

If you live in a warm climate and your remodeling project includes an addition or a roof replacement, choosing radiant barrier roof sheathing could be a wise choice. Radiant barriers can deflect up to 95% of solar radiation that strikes the house, thereby reducing the amount of heat the air-conditioning equipment would otherwise have to remove. In warm, sunny climates, radiant barriers can reduce cooling costs by as much as 10% to 15%.

UNDERSTANDING WINDOW PERFORMANCE

Several factors determine how well a particular window performs: how well it resists heat loss, how much solar radiation can pass through, how much visible light is admitted, and how resistant the window is to air infiltration and condensation. All new windows carry a label from the National Fenestration Rating Council (NFRC) that rates the window in each of the following categories.

U-Factor

Look for windows that have the lowest U-factor. The U-factor indicates the window's resistance to heat loss. The lower the number, the better the window prevents heat from escaping. (A window's U-factor is the inverse of its insulating value: $U = 1 / R\text{-value}$, so if the U-value is 0.35, $1 / 0.35 = R\text{-}2.86$.) In cold climates, you want the lowest U-factor possible. In warm climates, the U-factor is less important than the solar heat gain coefficient (SHGC).

Solar Heat Gain Coefficient

The SHGC (a number between 0 and 1) tells you how much of the sun's radiant heat can pass through the window. The lower the number, the less heat enters the house. In cold climates, you want a higher SHGC on south-facing windows to allow passive solar gain to warm your house—preferably above 0.5. In hot climates with significant air-conditioning needs, you want to reduce solar gain, so choose the lowest SHGC— preferably less than 0.4.

Visible Transmittance

Visible transmittance (VT) tells you how much visible light the window admits. The higher the number (usually from 0.3 to 0.8), the more daylight the window admits. In general, you want the highest VT. But if your primary concern is reducing solar gain, as may be the case in hot climates, the higher SHGC you'll need to prevent overheating will reduce the window's VT somewhat.

Air Leakage

Air leakage (AL) is responsible for convective heat loss. The more tightly the window is constructed, the less air leakage there will be. The AL score represents the amount of air, in cubic feet per minute, that can pass through 1 sq. ft. of window. Look for windows with an AL score below 0.3 (the range is from 0 to 1.0).

Condensation Resistance

Condensation resistance (CR) measures, on a scale of 0 to 100, how well the window resists condensation on its interior surfaces. The higher the window's CR rating, the more resistant it will be to the formation of condensation.

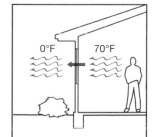
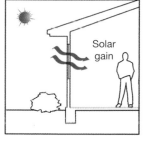
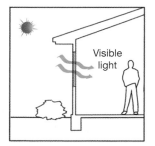
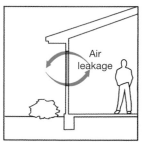

RADIANT BARRIER

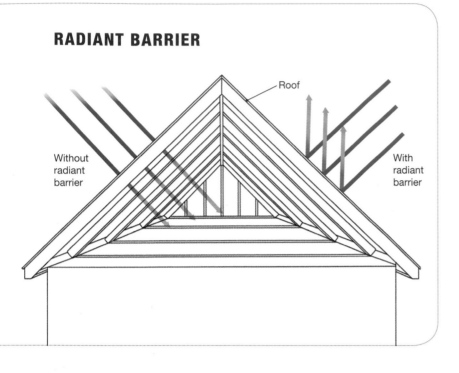

Roof

Without radiant barrier

With radiant barrier

Radiant barriers are typically a highly reflective material applied to the underside of the roof sheathing. Several manufacturers offer plywood and OSB sheathing with a thin sheet of aluminum bonded to one side. Other types of radiant barriers are available in rolls that can be applied from inside the attic to the underside of existing roofs. With either type, it is important to have an air space of at least 1 in. between the reflective surface of the radiant barrier and the insulation.

Roofing can also be used to deflect radiant heat. Light-colored roofs deflect heat, while dark roofs absorb heat. A white coating or membrane can be applied to an existing flat roof to reduce cooling loads, as opposed to the ubiquitous black roofing membranes that absorb solar radiation and force the air-conditioning to work overtime.

Some asphalt shingles are now made with a coating of reflective granules that will deflect 25% or more of the sun's heat. Metal roofs also reflect a lot of the sun's heat away from the house, which will reduce cooling costs. Although metal roofs are often more expensive than many other types, they are virtually maintenance free and extremely long lasting. The increased

▶ Radiant barriers are typically a highly reflective material applied to the underside of the roof sheathing.

▶▶ A white coating applied to the roof of this Harlem, New York, brownstone deflects the sun's heat, making it easier to keep the house cool in summer.

durability of a metal roof, combined with the reduced cooling costs from their high solar reflec-
tance, may make the extra cost a worthwhile investment.

Once we've created the most energy-efficient building envelope we can, reducing the
amount of heating and cooling required to keep the house comfortable to a minimum, it's time
to consider how we are going to provide that heating and cooling. In the next chapter, we'll take
a closer look at the mechanical systems that make up what I call the guts of a green remodel—
efficient heating and cooling systems, efficient water heating and water conservation, and lots of
ways to use less electricity.

**Metal roofs are
extremely long lasting,
virtually maintenance
free, and help keep the
house cool by deflect-
ing solar heat.**

ECODEEP HAUS

Kevin and Roxanne, both architects, wanted their family's home to be a model of sustainability. Ken's architectural firm, EcoDeep, specializes in green design, so he felt a special desire for his home to embody the vision he espouses to clients. They call the finished product the EcoDeep Haus.

Their purchase of a 1940s bungalow in St. Paul, Minnesota, embodied several green strategies right off the bat. Choosing to live in an established neighborhood meant that no new infrastructure (streets, sidewalks, water and sewer, and power lines) would need to be constructed to support their lifestyle. Finding a neighborhood with lots of amenities meant that they could walk everywhere. And, of course, the choice to remodel enabled them to reuse much of the existing house.

The decision to expand upward rather than outward eliminated the need for a large expanded foundation, with all the materials, energy, and expense that would entail. Instead, adding a second floor provided all the additional space they needed.

A patio at the rear of the house is made from bricks salvaged from walkways outside the original house.

PROJECT AT A GLANCE

Originally built: 1940

Original size: 1,700 sq. ft.

Size after remodel: 3,200 sq. ft.

Architect: Kevin Flynn, EcoDeep

Contractor: Michlitsch Builders

Location: St. Paul, Minnesota

SECOND FLOOR

Closet

Master bedroom

Bedroom

Bedroom

Bedroom

Balcony

FIRST FLOOR

Living room

Dining room

Mudroom

Kitchen

Pantry

Family room

Bedroom

Entry

BEFORE

AFTER

An integrated design process, which considers how all aspects of a project—design, materials, construction, and mechanical systems—affect each other, made it possible to double the living space in this award-winning remodel while cutting its energy bills in half.

LARGER HOUSE, SMALLER UTILITY BILLS

A multitude of green remodeling strategies employed to shrink the home's energy consumption have paid off in a big way. Although the completed house has nearly twice the living space, it uses 47% less electrical energy per square foot and 63% less natural gas per square foot than the original house did.

Strategies for reducing the home's energy demands include sprayed foam insulation for the roof and the new walls. Dense-pack cellulose was blown into the existing walls. To combat thermal bridging through the studs, a clip system was used to create an air space behind the siding. Generous south-facing windows allow for passive solar gain in winter, while sun shades made from sustainably harvested Ipe prevent unwanted solar gain in summer.

Super-high-performance windows with U-values in the 0.21 to 0.17 range (roughly R-5 to R-6) are "tuned" for maximum performance on each side of the house. On the north side, where preventing heat loss is the main concern, low-E coatings that reflect the most heat back into the house were chosen. To maximize passive solar heating in winter, coatings with a higher solar heat gain coefficient (that is, they admit more of the sun's radiant heat) were used for east-facing windows, and a still higher SHGC on the south side. On the west side, where afternoon sun can be intense, the windows have coatings engineered to reflect heat away from the glass.

Much of the energy the house does use is home generated. Solar hot water panels on the roof produce nearly all of the family's hot water needs from July to October and about half that in the winter. The solar photovoltaic panels produce an average of 25% of the home's annual electrical needs. (That figure would be closer to 50% if the energy demands of Kevin's home office were factored out.)

▲ Vegetated roofs offer a number of advantages. They double the life of the underlying roof membrane, reduce energy costs, manage storm-water runoff, soak up CO_2, and provide wildlife habitat.

▲▶ Viewed from above, the living room's polished concrete floor has radiant heating tubes embedded in it. Fly ash, a recycled material, was added to the concrete to reduce its carbon footprint.

▶ The floor of the balcony is made of Trex, a durable material made from a mixture of sawdust and recycled plastic. The sunshade above is Ipe, a sustainably harvested tropical hardwood.

UP ON THE ROOF

A white membrane covering exposed areas of the flat roof reduces the air-conditioning load by reflecting heat away from the house. (The lower AC load saves more energy than the heat gain of a dark roof would save during the heating season.) The white roof also reflects additional light onto some of the photovoltaic panels, giving them a slight efficiency boost.

A living green carpet covers most of the rest of the house. The owners were able to install the whole thing in six hours thanks to a vegetated roof system called LiveRoof® that comes in pre-planted modular trays. The plants, all native species, were selected for the home's specific exposure and microclimate, which in St. Paul means cold winters, months with lots of rain, and also extended dry periods. Except for periodic weeding, the green roof requires little maintenance.

Rainwater is harvested in rain barrels for use in landscape irrigation. Specially planted rain gardens (foreground) absorb excess storm-water runoff, reducing the burden on the neighborhood's storm drains.

▲ Oak flooring in the upstairs hall and sitting area was salvaged from two remodeled bedrooms.

▶ Energy Star–rated appliances in the kitchen save water and electricity. The apple-green quartz countertop is CaesarStone®, a durable, nontoxic material made by a company with a commitment to eco-friendly production practices.

DURABILITY IS GREEN

For the exterior, the owners wanted only materials that were durable and low maintenance. The house is sheathed in a combination of prefinished corrugated metal panels and cement board siding.

The front entry stair, back stair, and balcony flooring are made from Trex®, a composite material that's made from a mix of 50% reclaimed wood and sawdust and 50% recycled plastic bags. It contains none of the nasty chemicals found in pressure-treated pine, never needs sanding, painting, or staining, and doesn't splinter. The balcony facing and sunshades are made from Ipe, a highly durable and sustainable hardwood that resembles teak. Also known as Ironwood or Pau Lope, Ipe resists rot and insects and has a life expectancy of more than 40 years.

To conserve water, the house is fitted with low-flow plumbing fixtures and water-efficient appliances. Rain barrels collect rainwater for landscape irrigation. The owners expect to use 40% less water than the average home.

GREEN ON THE INSIDE

Four types of sustainable flooring were used inside the house. Locally harvested FSC-certified red oak was used in the kitchen and hallways. In the family room, cork, a rapidly renewable material, provides a slightly cushioned play surface for the children. The living and dining rooms have a polished concrete floor with radiant heat. Fly ash was added to the concrete to replace a portion of the high–embodied energy Portland cement.

Upstairs, oak flooring salvaged from some of the, reconfigured bedrooms was laid in the hallway. Flor™, a modular carpet system, was used in the kids' rooms. The formaldehyde-free carpet tiles have varying amounts of recycled content, contain antimicrobials that inhibit the growth of bacteria and mold, and meet the Carpet and Rug Institute's (CRI) Green Label Plus standards for VOC emissions.

Creating a healthy home for the family was a high priority. Zero-VOC paints and finishes were used throughout the house, and all of the adhesives used during construction were low-VOC products. To further enhance indoor environmental quality, fresh air is continuously supplied by an energy-recovery ventilation system equipped with high-efficiency pleated air filters that virtually eliminate airborne pollutants such as dust, mold spores, and pollen.

For Roxanne and Kevin, transforming an existing house into a comfortable, livable, and healthy home that was easy on the environment was both a labor of love and a sound financial investment. Interest in the award-winning project was so high that public tours were offered, and the house was filmed for the HGTV series *World's Greenest Houses*.

* Super-efficient windows with low-E coatings are "tuned" for each side of the house.

* High-performance sprayed foam insulation was used.

* Renewable energy from solar hot water and photovoltaic panels provides a significant portion of the total energy used.

* A vegetated roof adds insulation, manages storm water, soaks up CO_2, and provides a wildlife habitat.

* The appliances, furnace, and water heater are Energy Star rated.

* Highly durable exterior materials reduce maintenance.

A countertop made from recycled glass adds a splash of color to the second-floor hall bathroom.

5 THE GUTS OF A GREEN REMODEL

Once you've done everything you can do to reduce your home's heating and cooling loads—its appetite for heat and air-conditioning—it is time to consider exactly how to provide the smaller amount of space heating and cooling that you *will* need. In this chapter, we'll also discuss efficient ways to satisfy your home's water-heating requirements.

Remodeling provides a great opportunity to boost your home's energy performance. Improving the thermal characteristics of the building envelope, as we discussed in the last chapter, will reduce your home's appetite for energy; it won't require as many BTUs (British thermal units) of heating and cooling as a standard home, so your energy bills will be lower. And by creating that high-performance thermal envelope, you save money not only on energy costs for heating and cooling but also in other ways.

High-performance glazing minimizes heat loss through the expansive window walls of this sunny family room addition, keeping energy consumption low even during snowy Massachusetts winters. A similar addition with standard windows would require greater HVAC capacity.

TUNNELING THROUGH THE COST BARRIER

When your home requires fewer BTUs for heating and cooling, it doesn't require as large a system as a less well-insulated home. In really well-insulated homes, the HVAC system can be much smaller. Smaller equipment is less costly to purchase and to install.

This is where the concept of integrated design pays off big time. If you look at the cost of each individual improvement by itself, it may or may not seem to be cost-effective. But if you look at the big picture, you may get a very different answer. This is what Amory Lovens, the founder and director of the Rocky Mountain Institute, calls "tunneling through the cost barrier." In a nutshell, what he means is that making more radical thermal improvements to the building's shell can actually end up costing you less in the end.

If the scale of your renovation includes improvements to the entire building envelope, tunneling through the cost barrier might be just the ticket. This is where an investment in superior insulation, along with the highest-performing windows, can actually pay for itself at the get-go.

With a substantial enough reduction in heat loss at the home's perimeter, warm air could be supplied from the building's core rather than extending ductwork all the way to the exterior walls. And your HVAC system wouldn't need to produce nearly as many BTUs of heating or cooling, so it could be a lot smaller. In some cases, the savings from a smaller HVAC system with less ductwork can pay for most, if not all, of the cost of improvements to the shell.

With that in mind, it's time to focus on hardware, ducts, pipes, and various types of mechanical equipment—what I call the guts of a green remodel.

RIGHTSIZING YOUR HVAC SYSTEM

Maybe you've had this experience. You've decided to invest in a new air-conditioning system, and the contractor takes a look at your house, makes some measurements, and returns with recommendations for the size and type of system he wants to install. "It pencils out to about five tons of cooling," he tells you. "We're going to give you six, just to be safe. We don't believe in skimping. We want to make sure you're well covered."

Wrong! Don't listen to this kind of advice. Oversized equipment is always a mistake. Supersizing, the concept that more is better, has crept insidiously into our culture and even into the dictionary. (Do you want an extra-large popcorn for only 25 cents more?) If you're really hungry when you get to the movies, you might think that sounds like a good deal, but it's definitely the wrong way to go about sizing HVAC systems. More is not better. More is worse.

Here's why. Oversized HVAC systems produce hot air that is too hot and cold air that is too cold to make your house truly comfortable. The system pumps out too much overly warm or overly cool air too quickly. This satisfies the thermostat too fast. Then the equipment shuts off. No matter how well insulated the house is, once the system shuts off the house gradually (or in some houses, not so gradually) begins to lose or gain heat. As soon as the temperature varies from the thermostat set point by a couple of degrees, the system kicks in again.

This happens over and over again. It's called short-cycling. The system turning itself on and off more frequently than it should creates undue wear and tear, causing more frequent

green view

Spending money on things you can't see can be a wise investment. If your remodeling project includes new heating and air-conditioning equipment, spend money first on air sealing, insulation, and high-performance windows.

A home with a nearly airtight, well-insulated shell will have much more modest needs for heating and air-conditioning. This lower demand means your heating and cooling equipment will be cheaper to run and, because energy use is reduced, so is your carbon footprint. But there are even greater savings to be had because whatever new equipment you buy will be smaller. And the lower cost of a smaller heating and cooling plant will make a big dent in the improvements to the home's thermal envelope in the first place.

◄◄ Just right. Using Manual J heat-loss calculations, the ultra-high-efficiency 23-SEER air conditioner was sized to precisely match the reduced cooling loads of this exceptionally well-insulated green remodel. Even during sultry New Orleans summers, keeping the interior cool and comfortable doesn't run up high electric bills.

maintenance issues and shortening its useful life. And because it never runs for a long time during any cycle, it never runs at peak efficiency. So if you have, for example, a boiler that's rated at 85% efficiency, it may only perform at 65% to 70% efficiency if it's short-cycling. That means money is going up the chimney.

Another disadvantage of oversized HVAC systems is that your house will be less comfortable. A system that pumps out air that is either too warm or too cold will produce uneven heating or cooling. You'll have some areas that are too warm and others that are too cold. And since heat always moves from warmer areas to cooler areas, this will also produce drafts.

What we want is a system that is neither oversized nor undersized but one that is *rightsized*. We could call this the Goldilocks school of thermodynamics. We want a system that is not too big, not too small, but sized just right for our house.

Heat-loss calculations

So what does it mean to have a rightsized system? To answer that question, it is necessary to understand something about how heating and cooling capacity is determined. The most important thing that an engineer or contractor needs to size your system is a heat-loss calculation. Doing this accurately enough to account for all the variables requires what is called a Manual J residential load calculation. This takes into account the total surface area of the building envelope, what it is made of, and which way it is facing. South-facing windows, because they admit direct sunlight, need to be calculated differently than windows facing north, for example.

Different parts of the building are made of different materials. As we discussed in chapter 4, various types of materials allow heat to pass through them at different rates. The R-value for most windows is only in the 2 to 3 range. That keeps the wind out but doesn't do a lot to prevent conductive heat loss. And depending on how a wall is constructed and insulated, a 2x6 wall

WHAT IS A MANUAL J CALCULATION?

A Manual J residential load calculation is the method recommended by the Air Conditioning Contractors of America (ACCA) for sizing HVAC equipment. A Manual J calculation measures heat loss through walls, ceilings, windows, and doors. It takes into account wall thickness and materials; type and condition of insulation; total floor area and ceiling height; number, size, and type of windows; heat gain from sunlight entering the building; body heat given off by people; and the heat emitted by lights and appliances. Weather conditions for the area, building orientation and exposure, and even landscape features that produce shade or help block the wind are also used as inputs for the load calculations. Although it is possible to do this with pencil and paper, today most contractors use Manual J software to arrive at the most accurate results.

All of these factors contribute to the rates at which the house will lose or gain heat under various weather conditions at different seasons and times of day. Once the numbers are crunched, the result tells the contractor exactly how many BTUs of heating and cooling are required to maintain the house at a comfortable temperature all year round.

Rule-of-thumb load calculations don't apply. The high-performance building envelope of this remodeled duplex in Cambridge, Massachusetts, employs a continuous exterior layer of rigid foam insulation, resulting in heating and cooling loads 38% lower than conventional homes. The rightsized HVAC system is therefore smaller, less costly, and more economical to operate.

could have an effective R-value of anywhere from 9 to more than 30. So it is essential to know how the wall is constructed and insulated. Is it built with 2x4s or 2x6s? Are the studs spaced 16 in. on center (o.c.) or 24 in. o.c.? (Remember, wider spacing allows for more insulation.) What kind of insulation was used, and how well was it installed?

By making reasonably accurate assumptions about how the walls are built and then calculating the total surface area of each type of material, it is then possible to arrive at the rate at which the house will lose or gain heat under various conditions. For example, more heat is lost through windows than through solid walls. But sunlight entering through south-facing windows can help warm a home's interior. If the sunlight falls on a material with thermal mass, like concrete, stone, or tile, or even walls with a double layer of drywall, that thermal mass will absorb heat from the sun and then release it slowly after the sun has set. All that has to be taken into account to understand a home's thermal characteristics.

Assumptions also have to be made about the rate of air infiltration—leaky homes lose heat much faster than tightly sealed homes. Even the fact that doors are opened whenever someone enters or exits has to be factored in as well. Whatever the scope of your remodeling project, it should definitely include sealing air leaks in the entire house (see chapter 4).

Climate also plays a role. The greater the difference between the temperature on the inside and on the outside of the wall, the greater the rate of heat loss will be. So the engineer needs to know the average daily temperatures in your geographical area for different times of year. Wind is a factor, too. If your house is in a particularly windy location, its rate of heat loss will be greater, so that needs to be factored into the heat-loss calculations as well.

Sizing for design days Armed with all that information, it is possible to make a reasonable prediction about how much heating or cooling your house will need at different times of year. Generally, the heating system will be sized to cope with the coldest winter day that can normally be expected in your area, and the AC system will be sized to cope with the hottest day of summer. These two extremes of temperature are called the "design days," in other words, the most difficult days your system will be designed to handle for both heating and cooling.

Now, here is where many HVAC contractors get into trouble. It's that common assumption that more is better. (More of some things frequently *is* better—chocolate, for example—but not necessarily BTUs.) You don't want a system capable of turning your house into a meat locker in the summer or a sauna in the winter. What you want, instead, is a system that is designed to run more or less continuously on the design days. You want your heat to run most of the time on the coldest day of winter, which will provide steady, draft-free warmth, and you want your air-conditioning to run most of the time on the hottest day of the summer. This will dehumidify the air without making the house uncomfortably cold. In winter and summer, a rightsized system will provide the most comfortable, even temperatures throughout the house and enable your system to operate at peak efficiency.

Performance specifications

Contracts for HVAC installations often include performance specs. The size of the system is calculated in BTUs, but that doesn't really tell you much about how well it will perform in your house. Performance specs tell you exactly what you can expect the system to do—how it will perform—under certain conditions. The contract may state, for example, that the system will be sufficient to maintain the home's indoor temperature at 70°F degrees when the outdoor temperature is 0°F, and at 74°F when the outdoor temperature is 100°F. (This will obviously vary from one climatic zone to another.)

How will the heat generated by your new, efficient HVAC equipment get to where you want it? The options fall into two main categories: convection and radiation. Furnaces use convection; they distribute warm air around the house through ductwork. In radiant systems, heat is supplied by a boiler that sends hot water to baseboard or wall-mounted radiators or to tubing installed beneath a floor (see the drawing on p. 110). Hydro-air systems combine both methods. Hot water produced by a boiler is piped to one or more air handlers, where a fan blows air over a coil of copper tubing. The moving air picks up the heat from the coil and distributes it to each room through the same kind of ductwork used with furnaces.

Hot water tubing just below the finished floor of this Seattle remodel provides gentle, draft-free radiant heating. The warm floors concentrate most of the heat in the zone occupied by people rather than up near the ceiling, so thermostats can be set lower.

Performance specs are a good thing. It is much better to have a contract that guarantees your house will be 70°F inside when it is 0°F outside than one that just tells you how many BTUs the system will put out. You can't be expected to know how many BTUs you need. A contract that shows that you got all the BTUs you paid for won't keep you warm in the winter or cool in the summer.

HVAC OPTIONS

Not every remodeling project entails making changes to the home's HVAC system. In smaller projects that are primarily about sprucing up or reconfiguring existing space, you probably won't be replacing the existing mechanical equipment, especially if it is in relatively good condition and not nearing the end of its useful life. In that case, you might just consider a minor tune-up by a qualified service professional and having leaky ductwork sealed.

But if your remodel increases the amount of finished living space, or if your current HVAC system is old or in poor condition, you will likely end up replacing the old equipment to meet the heating and cooling demands of the remodeled home. But how do you decide what to replace it with? Here are some options.

Gas, oil, or electric?

The vast majority of homes in the United States are heated with gas, oil, or electricity. The choice most often depends on which is available in a particular location. But whichever fuel your home uses, you want to use as little of it as possible.

The performance of combustion heating equipment—that is, furnaces and boilers—is measured by its annual fuel utilization efficiency (AFUE) rating. The minimum AFUE for new furnaces sold today is 78%, which means that it converts 78% of the energy contained in the fuel to heat. But for a green remodel, you shouldn't even think about equipment that isn't Energy Star rated. To wear the Energy Star label, a furnace or boiler must have an AFUE of at least 85%. But why stop there? Today you can find boilers with efficiency ratings as high as 95% and furnaces with an AFUE of up to 98%. Models rated at 90% and above are called condensing furnaces or boilers, which means they capture some of the heat that normally escapes up the chimney by condensing escaping water vapor. (See the chart on p. 111 to find out what kind of return you can expect on your investment based on the efficiency of the new unit compared with the old one.)

Electric heating Electric resistance heat is 100% efficient—it converts all, or nearly all, of the energy in the electricity to heat. But the cost of electricity makes this the least economical choice.

Electric heat pumps, though, can produce twice as much heat (or more) per kilowatt hour (kWh) of electricity as resistance heaters, making them a viable alternative in parts of the country with moderate heating and cooling needs. In colder climates, however, heat pumps have to work harder to extract heat from the frigid air, so their efficiency drops off steeply.

As the name implies, heat pumps move heat from one place to another. In winter, air-source heat pumps move the residual heat contained in the cold outside air to the inside of your house, much as your refrigerator's compressor removes heat from inside the appliance and expels it into your kitchen. This is why you feel warm air coming out of the bottom of your refrigerator.

While air-source heat pumps are unsuitable for very cold climates, ground-source heat pumps, also known as water-source or geothermal heat pumps, extract heat from below ground where the temperature is close to 50°F year-round. Although more expensive to install than other systems, the high operating efficiency of geothermal heat pumps often makes them an economical choice in the long run.

Even the most efficient geothermal systems, however, still run on electricity. In most parts of the country, electricity is produced by burning fossil fuels, a major source of greenhouse gas emissions. As most fossil fuel power plants operate at 30% to 40% efficiency, even the most efficient use of electricity still produces CO_2 emissions.

An evacuated-tube solar hot water collector coupled with two 168-gallon insulated storage tanks meet the space heating and domestic hot water needs for a net-zero energy remodel in Boulder, Colorado.

Solar heating Heating with a solar hot water system, on the other hand, produces no CO_2 at all. (Most solar thermal systems do employ small electric pumps, but the amount of electricity consumed is miniscule compared with any other method of space heating.) If you have a section of south-facing roof that's not in the shadow of trees or other buildings, solar thermal is worth considering. Depending on the size of the installation, it could provide most, if not all, of your domestic hot water needs, or warm water for radiant space heating. In most cases, you will still need a backup heat source for times when sunshine is scarce. But solar thermal systems offer attractive payback scenarios for many homeowners.

HEAT DISTRIBUTION

CONVECTION SYSTEM

A convection system distributes warm or cool air throughout the house. For space heating, the warm air can be supplied by a furnace that heats air directly; by a hybrid hydronic system, which distributes hot water to one or more fan coil units (air handlers); or by a water-to-air ground-source heat pump.

HYDRONIC SYSTEM

A hydronic heating system distributes hot water from a boiler, heat pump, or solar water heater to provide radiant heating, either through radiators or loops of PEX tubing below the floor.

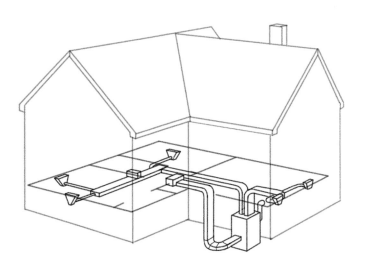

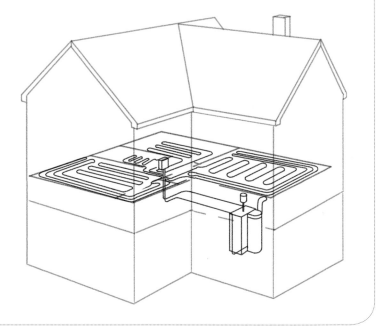

Conventional upgrades

Often the most convenient option is to upgrade to a more efficient version of whatever system you already have. So, if your existing system uses an oil-fired boiler, upgrading to a more efficient boiler or replacing the boiler's oil burner with a more efficient one will reduce your fuel bills. Likewise, replacing an old gas-fired furnace with a high-efficiency model makes sense for many homes, and the financial payback can be quite attractive. And by switching to a more efficient system, you will also reduce your greenhouse gas emissions. This is a very good thing. But is it the very best thing?

Geothermal systems

I might as well just come out and say it—nothing beats geothermal HVAC systems in terms of efficiency. I'm a big fan of geothermal. If the scope of your remodel allows for a completely new HVAC system, you might do well to consider going the geothermal route. While upgrading your furnace or boiler might improve your efficiency by 50%, switching to a geothermal system can boost your efficiency by 300% or more.

CALCULATING THE RETURN ON INVESTMENT FOR A NEW HEATING SYSTEM

If you know the AFUE (Annual Fuel Utilization Efficiency) rating for your boiler or furnace, you can estimate the savings from replacing it with a newer, more efficient model by using the chart at right. If you don't know the AFUE of your old system, you can get a good enough rule-of-thumb figure from the table below, compiled by the U.S. Department of Energy.

First, find the row at left that matches the AFUE of your existing system, and then find the column that matches the AFUE of the new system. The value where the two intersect is the annual dollar savings per $100 of energy cost.

So if, for example, your old furnace has an AFUE of 60% and the replacement you are considering has an AFUE of 95%, your estimated savings is $37 for every $100 of current fuel expense. If your current annual heating bill is $2,500, your annual savings will be 25 x $37 = $925.

Then divide the cost of the new system by the annual savings. So if the new system costs $5,000, then $925 ÷ $5,000 = 18.5% ROI. That's a pretty good return for any investment. And as the price of fuel rises, so do your savings.

You should also consider how this investment affects the value of your house. Most home buyers would expect to pay less for a home with a 20-year-old boiler than they would for a home with a relatively new one because they know the older boiler will need replacing one day in the near future.

SAVINGS PER $100 OF HEATING BILL

AFUE OF NEW SYSTEM

AFUE OF EXISTING SYSTEM	80%	85%	90%	95%
50%	$37	$41	$44	$47
55%	$31	$35	$38	$42
60%	$25	$29	$33	$37
65%	$19	$23	$27	$32
70%	$12	$18	$22	$26
75%	$6	$11	$17	$21
80%	—	$6	$11	$16
85%	—	—	$6	$11

Adapted from ACEEE.org

TYPICAL AFUE RATINGS FOR DIFFERENT TYPES OF FURNACES AND BOILERS

TYPE	PRE-1960	1960–1969	1970–1974	1975–1983	1984–1987	1988–1991	POST-1992
Gas furnace	60%	60%	65%	65%	68%	76%	78%
Gas boiler	60%	60%	65%	65%	70%	77%	80%
Oil furnace	60%	65%	72%	75%	80%	80%	80%
Oil boiler	60%	65%	72%	75%	80%	80%	80%

The one downside to geothermal systems is the relatively high initial cost. A geothermal installation is likely to cost two to two and a half times as much as a conventional system. But because these systems are so efficient, the incremental up-front costs will eventually be recouped by the resulting energy cost savings. The real question is, how long will that take? The answer is, it depends. The main variables are the cost of electricity in your area, the type of system you are replacing, and how well your house is insulated. And don't forget to find out what utility company rebates and government tax incentives are available in your area. A comprehensive state-by-state database of incentives can be found at www.dsireusa.org.

Also known as ground-source heat pumps, or geo-exchange systems, geothermal systems operate on the same principle as air-to-air heat pumps but more efficiently. And since groundwater temperature is relatively constant, the efficiency of geothermal systems doesn't vary, while the efficiency of air-source heat pumps fluctuates with the outdoor temperature. Both air-source and ground-source heat pumps provide heating and cooling.

How does a geothermal system work? Furnaces and boilers create heat by burning fossil fuels, but geothermal systems don't need combustion. Instead, they simply move heat from one place to another. Water circulating through one or more wells or a buried loop of plastic tubing, or refrigerant

A direct-exchange geothermal system, also known as a ground-source heat pump, provides highly efficient heating and air-conditioning for this LEED Platinum remodel in Ann Arbor, Michigan.

circulating through buried copper tubing, carries the earth's heat into the home to a geothermal heat pump (also known as a ground-source or water-source pump). The pump uses compressors and heat exchangers in a vapor compression cycle—the same principle employed in a refrigerator—to concentrate the earth's energy and distribute the heat to the home's interior.

In summer, the process is reversed to provide air-conditioning. Heat is drawn from the home, expelled to the loop, and absorbed by the earth. This is exactly the same way a refrigerator keeps its contents cold—by extracting heat from the interior and moving it somewhere else. The warm air you feel blowing from the bottom of your refrigerator was extracted from its interior.

While ordinary air-conditioning compressors draw excess heat from inside your home and expel it to the air outdoors, geothermal heat pumps can be located indoors because they exchange heat with the ground instead of the air.

Unlike conventional air-source heat pumps that need to work harder to draw heat from the air when the temperature drops, ground-source heat pumps draw heat from a highly stable source—the earth—so they use less electricity. The temperature of the ground a few feet beneath the surface remains within a relatively narrow range throughout the year, in most areas around 50°F.

Geothermal installations that use a well are known as in-direct, or open-loop, systems. A closed-loop system circulates water through plastic tubing buried in the ground. Both systems employ a heat exchanger to transfer heat from the water to the geothermal heat pump. Direct exchange (DX) systems circulate refrigerant through copper tubes buried deep in the ground. The refrigerant absorbs heat from the earth and transfers it directly to the heat pump.

GEOTHERMAL SYSTEMS

VERTICAL SYSTEM

In vertical closed-loop systems, pipes are inserted into multiple boreholes that average from 150 ft. to 250 ft. in depth per ton of equipment. The number of boreholes depends on the home's heating load.

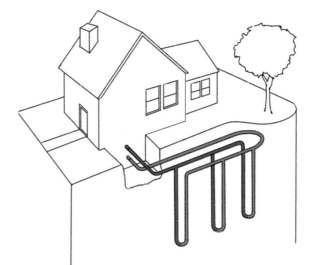

HORIZONTAL SYSTEM

Horizontal loops are an economical choice if you have enough land. On average, horizontal systems require 300 ft. to 600 ft. of piping for every ton of capacity.

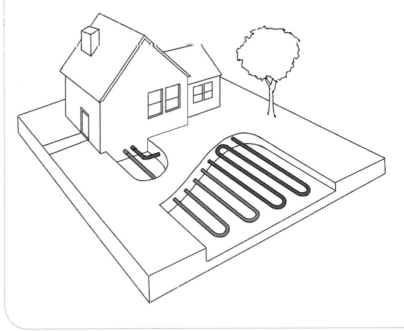

Geothermal water heating Geothermal systems can also provide all or part of a home's hot water through the addition of a desuperheater. A desuperheater is an auxiliary heat exchanger that uses superheated gases from the heat pump's compressor to heat water.

In summer, when the system is in the cooling mode, the desuperheater uses the excess heat that would otherwise be expelled to the ground, so domestic hot water is essentially free. But a conventional water heater is still needed to boost temperature in winter when the desuperheater isn't producing enough, and in spring and fall when the system may be turned off in favor of open windows.

INDIRECT WATER HEATER

Indirect water heaters use a heat exchanger to transfer the heat produced by another device, typically a space-heating boiler, into an insulated storage tank.

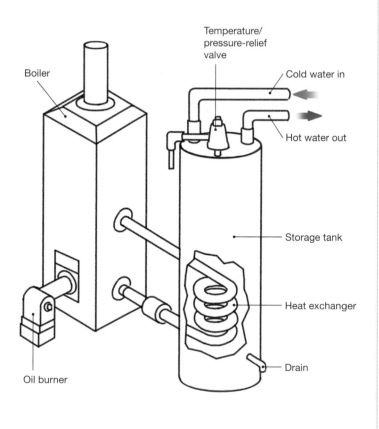

Boiler

Temperature/ pressure-relief valve

Cold water in

Hot water out

Storage tank

Heat exchanger

Drain

Oil burner

Adapted from www.energysavers.gov

Cogeneration units, such as Honda's Micro-sized Combined Heat and Power (MCHP) Deluxe paired with ECR International's freewatt™ system, generate electricity and capture the waste heat to supplement water or space heating in your home. They provide the most benefit in regions with long winters and low natural gas prices.

Geothermal systems are typically more expensive to install than conventional systems, but the exceptionally low operating costs more than make up for the extra expenditure within a few years. According to the U.S. Environmental Protection Agency, geothermal systems save home-owners 30% to 70% in heating costs and 20% to 50% in cooling costs compared with conventional systems. They also require less maintenance than conventional systems.

Other systems on the horizon

Two new technologies that are likely to have applications for home use in the future are cogeneration, also known as combined heat and power (CHP) systems, and fuel cells. Combined heat and power systems are essentially generators that run on propane or natural gas. They capture the waste heat they produce and make it available for space and water heating. Large CHP systems have been in use in factories and large buildings for some time, but residential-sized units, referred to as micro CHP, or MCHP, are rare. The economics of residential CHP systems vary greatly. They are most cost-effective in areas where electricity is expensive relative to natural gas or propane and in areas with long winters, where the captured waste heat can be used for more of the year. One commercial device currently on the market is the Micro-sized Combined Heat and Power (MCHP) Deluxe cogeneration unit from Honda (see the photo on the facing page).

Fuel cells produce electricity by combining hydrogen and oxygen. The by-products of the electrochemical reaction are water and heat. As with CHP units, the heat from fuel cell power generation can be used for home heating. In theory, it sounds great. In practice, residential fuel cells have a long way to go before they can be widely and economically implemented. It's definitely a technology to watch, but not one likely to show up in green remodels anytime soon.

GETTING INTO HOT WATER

Domestic hot water, the water we use for bathing, laundry, dishwashing, and cooking, consumes from 15% to 25% of the energy used in a typical single-family home. When you're remodeling, this is an easy place to save money, water, and energy all at the same time.

The first way to save on hot water is simply to use less of it. Just as in our discussion of efficient space heating, the first thing you want to do is reduce demand. We'll talk more about conserving water in the next chapter, but for now, the sidebar on p. 116 will give you several ideas for ways to reduce your total hot water consumption. For smaller projects, such as kitchen or bathroom remodels, that might be all you need to know about hot water. But if your plans include upgrading your water heater, read on.

EFFICIENCY RATINGS FOR AIR-CONDITIONING SYSTEMS

SEER ratings for air conditioners are a little like fuel-efficiency ratings for cars. If your car has an EPA rating of 30 miles per gallon (mpg), you'll only get 30 mpg if you drive at 55 miles per hour on a relatively flat road. The faster you drive, the lower your actual mileage will be. Likewise, if your air conditioner is rated at 13 SEER, it will only perform at that level of efficiency within a certain temperature range. The unit's efficiency falls off as the outdoor temperature rises. When it is 90°F outside, that 13-SEER unit's efficiency will be closer to 11.5. At 95°F the efficiency will fall to 10, and if the temperature rises to 110°F, the unit will only perform at a SEER of about 8.25.

By contrast, a geothermal system in air-conditioning mode has an energy efficiency rating of about 18 regardless of the outdoor air temperature because it is exchanging heat with the relatively unvarying temperature of the earth.

10 WAYS TO CUT YOUR WATER-HEATING BILLS

Water heating accounts for up to 25% of the energy consumed in your home. You can reduce your monthly water-heating bills by selecting an efficient water heater and implementing some simple strategies for reducing your domestic hot water usage.

1. Use Energy Star–rated dishwashers and clothes washers, which use less water than conventional models.

2. Wash only full loads of dishes and clothes.

3. Take showers instead of baths. Filling a bathtub uses more hot water than an average shower.

4. Take shorter showers—even shaving one minute off your daily shower will save quite a bit of energy. Try using a five-minute egg timer to limit your shower time. Showering accounts for 37% of hot water usage in the average home.

5. Switch to low-flow showerheads. Using less water means heating less water. An average family can save hundreds of dollars per year in energy costs.

6. Install a drain-water heat-recovery system, which can save 25% to 30% of water-heating costs.

7. Insulate the hot water pipes connected to the water heater.

8. Insulate your natural gas or oil hot-water storage tank (but be careful not to cover the water heater's top, bottom, thermostat, or burner compartment).

9. Lower the thermostat on your water heater to 120°F.

10. Repair leaks. A dripping faucet can cause your water heater to work overtime and cost you money.

HOT WATER USAGE
Showers account for 37% of the hot water used in an average home. Using less water for showers means heating less water. Low-flow showerheads save not only water but also quite a bit of energy.

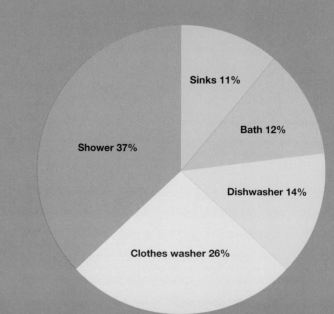

Sinks 11%

Bath 12%

Shower 37%

Dishwasher 14%

Clothes washer 26%

◂▴ In addition to providing hot water for cooking and washing, the high-efficiency water heater in this well-insulated Harlem, New York, brownstone remodel also doubles as the heat source for the radiant-heated floors throughout the house.

Your choice of a water heater will often be determined by the type of heating system you have in your home. If you have a hydronic system—in other words, one that uses hot water to heat your home—adding an indirect water heater can be an economical choice, especially if you have a high-efficiency boiler. If you have a gas furnace, you'll want to consider either a high-efficiency conventional water heater or a demand (tankless) water heater. If your house is all electric, then a heat pump water heater might be right for you. Solar water heaters, of course, can be used no matter what your fuel source.

In some cases, an efficient water heater can supply your space heating as well as hot water for cooking and washing. If your home is heated with hot water and you've succeeded in reduc-

▲◄ **Heat pump water heaters concentrate ambient heat from the surrounding air with a compressor to heat water more than twice as efficiently as a standard electric unit. Aftermarket units, such as the AirTap, can be added to existing tanks. You can also buy all-in-one heat pump water heaters from a variety of manufacturers.**

▲▶ **Tankless, also known as demand, water heaters produce hot water only while being used. When a tap is opened, the flow of water triggers the burner to light and continuously heat water until the tap is closed.**

ing your home's space-heating needs sufficiently, you may be able to dispense with a separate boiler altogether.

Water heater options

There are lots of things you can do to save money on your water-heating bills (see the sidebar on p. 116), but let's also take a look at the most efficient ways to produce that hot water. If you just want to replace your hot water heater, look for the Energy Star label and find the one with the lowest annual energy cost. Choosing a power-vented or sealed combustion model will also eliminate any chance of combustion gases mixing with your indoor air supply.

Tankless water heaters make a lot of sense in certain applications because they heat water only as it is being used. They use less energy because there is no storage tank to keep hot. And they can be a great space saver in smaller homes where storage space is at a premium. The units themselves are usually more expensive than traditional storage-type water heaters, but the energy and space savings can make them an attractive option. Tankless heaters are particularly well suited to second homes that are used primarily on weekends or left unoccupied for much of the year, where it makes little sense to maintain a tank of hot water that no one is using.

If your plans call for a geothermal system for space heating and cooling, the same equipment can produce hot water economically. But you will still need an auxiliary hot water source for times when no heat or air-conditioning is being called for.

The newest entries into the water-heating market are heat pump, or hybrid, water heaters. There are stand-alone models as well as an ingenious product called the AirTap™ that can be retrofitted to an existing storage-type water heater as a replacement for the existing heat source. The AirTap functions just like a conventional heat pump, using a compressor (powered by a low-wattage electric current) to extract heat from the surrounding air and then sending this heat through long copper tubes into an adapter, where it is dispersed in your water tank.

Solar Water Heaters There are two basic types of solar water heaters: passive and active. Passive systems have no moving parts; they rely on the principle that hot water rises and cold water falls. These are best suited for locales with little or no risk of freezing. Active, or forced circulation, systems employ a small circulating pump and a controller.

In both systems, a solar collector, usually on the roof, is connected to a hot water storage tank inside the house. And, in most cases, the tank has a backup heat source to meet demand when sunshine is limited.

Rooftop solar collectors fall into two main categories: glazed, flat plate collectors, and evacuated tubes. The first type consists of a flat copper plate, painted black, inside of a glazed, insulated box. Solar energy absorbed by the plate is transferred to water flowing through tubes inside the box. In evacuated tube collectors, an antifreeze solution flows through absorption pipes inside of glass vacuum tubes, which minimize heat loss. Evacuated tube systems are more expensive, but also more efficient. Efficient space heating and water heating will save you money and reduce your home's environmental footprint. But reducing your total water usage has its own virtues. In the next chapter, we'll look more closely at ways of saving both water and electricity.

CHOOSING A WATER HEATER

If your remodeling plans include a new water heater, there are several types to choose from:

Conventional storage water heaters: These are insulated storage tanks with their own internal heat source, either gas, oil, or electric.

Indirect water heaters: Indirect water heaters use a heat exchanger to transfer the heat produced by another device, typically a space-heating boiler, into an insulated storage tank.

Tankless, or demand, water heaters: Tankless water heaters have no storage tank, and they provide continuous hot water only when called for.

Heat pump water heaters: Also known as hybrid electric water heaters, these draw heat from the surrounding air to heat water in a storage tank. They are twice as efficient as standard electric water heaters.

Solar water heaters: Indirect systems circulate antifreeze heat-transfer fluid through the collectors and a heat exchanger inside an insulated storage tank. Direct systems circulate the home's water supply directly through the collectors. These are recommended only for climates not prone to freezing.

A LEED PLATINUM REMODEL IN MICHIGAN

A total gut job: The original 1870 structure was stripped down to the studs, with much of the original sheathing left intact. A later structure at the back of the house was demolished to make way for the new addition.

When John and Karen decided to get married, one of the first decisions they had to make was where to live. John owned a modest 19th-century frame house in the Kerrytown district of Ann Arbor, Michigan, but it had problems: It was tired, drafty, and expensive to heat. On the plus side, the house had charm and was located in a diverse, lively neighborhood of tree-shaded streets, within walking distance of shops, restaurants, theaters, a farmers' market, and nearly everything else the two of them would need on a daily basis.

Looking for a new house would have been an easy decision, but the location offered so many advantages that they decided to take on a complete gut renovation of John's house while living in a rented apartment down the street. Having already made a commitment to biking instead of driving whenever possible, the couple wanted to reduce their home's dependence on fossil fuels, too. Karen started reading up on geothermal systems; the extreme energy efficiency they offered appealed strongly to her green sensibilities. So when they began interviewing contractors, finding someone with geothermal experience was a priority. When they met Doug Selby of Meadowlark Builders, they knew the search was over. Doug and his partner Kirk Brandon had developed a core expertise in green building and had installed a number of geothermal systems.

In the backyard, a small patch of grass surrounded by mulched planting beds minimizes the need for water, pesticides, and fertilizers—not to mention lawn mowing.

FIRST FLOOR (BEFORE)

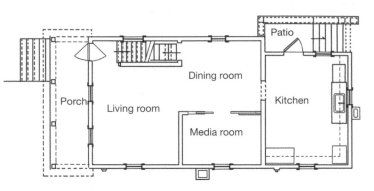

FIRST FLOOR (AFTER)

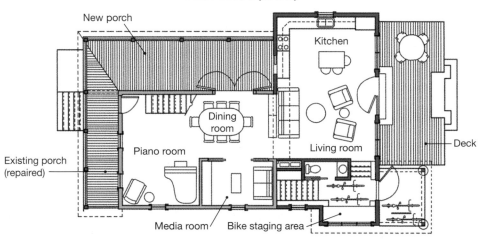

A copper rain chain funnels runoff from the roof into a specially planted rain garden that captures storm water and allows it to percolate slowly into the ground. The permeable driveway also serves to minimize runoff from the site.

INTEGRATED DESIGN

Doug introduced John and Karen to Michael Klement, whose firm, Architectural Resources, specializes in sustainable design. It was a good fit; the client, architect, and contractor fell into a congenial working relationship that fostered an integrated design approach that considered how each part of the house affected the whole. Together they would assess each decision in terms of reducing energy use, conserving natural resources, making efficient use of limited space to minimize the building's impact (and keep costs down), and providing the healthiest possible indoor air quality.

Creating an extremely well-insulated shell was a high priority; the entire structure was insulated with sprayed-in-place open-cell foam. The foundation for the addition at the rear of the house was constructed with insulated concrete forms. And 2 in. of rigid foam insulation was laid beneath the new basement slab. A reflective standing-seam metal roof was selected to deflect the summer sun to reduce cooling loads. The reduced heating and cooling demands are met by a direct-exchange geothermal heat pump.

◄◄ With no alteration except cleaning up, the beams become the legs of a custom dining table, where their rough-hewn character offers a sharp contrast to the sleek steel and glass top.

▲► A crystal-clear column of water from a ceiling-mounted, laminar-flow tub filler pours into a Japanese soaking tub made from recycled stainless steel. The deep, small-diameter tub has room for two and retains heat longer than conventional tubs. The vanity's countertop is PaperStone, made from recycled paper.

As in any tightly sealed home, ventilation was essential; an energy-recovery ventilator provides eight complete air changes per day while conserving 85% of the heat from the exhaust air stream. To further enhance indoor air quality, the ventilation system is equipped with high-efficiency air filters. All interior materials and finishes were selected for the lowest possible levels of harmful chemicals.

CONSERVING WATER, MANAGING WASTE

To conserve water, John and Karen selected ultralow-flow plumbing fixtures, fed by PEX tubing. Because PEX is flexible, there are no joints or right angles that create friction and slow down the flow of water, so the tubes can have a smaller diameter than copper lines. For that reason, hot water, supplied by a tankless water heater, is delivered to each point of use faster, saving energy and reducing the amount of water that is normally wasted while waiting for it to heat up. Outdoor water use was minimized by limiting the amount of lawn and choosing drought-tolerant, native plantings. Rain barrels capture runoff from the roof to use for watering flower beds.

Managing waste was something Meadowlark Builders now did routinely. Recycling, careful ordering, and reuse of materials diverted 75% of construction waste from landfills. Most of the lumber from tearing out an old addition at the back of the house was reused in the finished

* Staying small:

  • Careful space planning and a few *Not So Big House* strategies make every square inch count. All of the owners' needs were fit into a 1,850-sq.-ft., four-bedroom package.

* Water efficiency is achieved by:

  • Limiting turf and choosing drought-tolerant plantings.

  • Harvesting rainwater.

  • Installing ultralow-flow plumbing fixtures.

* Energy efficiency: The estimated cost for heating and cooling the house is $26 per month.

  • Sprayed-foam insulation creates a tight thermal envelope.

  • The fully insulated attic keeps ductwork inside the conditioned space, increasing both heating and cooling efficiency.

  • The basement slab is insulated with 2 in. of rigid foam under the concrete.

  • The home uses direct-exchange geothermal heating and cooling.

  • Energy Star appliances were installed.

  • An induction cooktop is the most energy-efficient way to cook.

* Environmentally preferable products were used.

  • Countertops are made from recycled paper.

  • Fly ash in the concrete replaces 30% of portland cement, diverting waste from landfills and reducing the embodied energy of the concrete.

* Reclaimed materials:

  • All lumber from demolished walls was reused for framing new walls and even for decorative elements like interior windowsills.

  • The stair treads are made from lumber the contractor salvaged when renovating an old theater down the block and stored for just such an occasion.

* Indoor environmental quality is maintained through the use of:

  • Radon-resistant construction.

  • A MERV-10 air-filtration system.

  • No fireplace (most fireplaces suck more heat out of a house than they produce and can also cause air-quality issues).

Soft, even light from a skylight with a splayed light well illuminates an exercise/yoga space upstairs, and filters down the stairwell where a light-colored wall reflects the daylight into the first floor.

renovation. All of the new lumber used in the addition was FSC certified. Advanced framing techniques (see chapter 7) reduced the amount of lumber in the addition's walls, providing space for 20% more insulation.

As the design phase drew to its conclusion, Klement decided, just for fun, to compare the choices they had made to the LEED for Homes checklist. To his surprise, without having tried to comply with any written green building standard, the home would qualify for LEED Platinum certification. Not only that, but this would be the first LEED Platinum remodel in Michigan.

▲ The bright new kitchen has Energy Star–rated appliances and cabinets made from formaldehyde-free plywood and low-VOC adhesives and finish. The LED recessed lights use even less electricity than CFLs, contain no mercury, and are expected to last 20 years.

◀ The bike staging area, high on the wish list for the biking-enthusiast homeowners, doubles as a mudroom. The windowsills are made of lumber reclaimed from the demolished portion of the original house.

6 SAVING WATER AND ELECTRICITY

The previous chapter dipped a toe into the subject of water—but more specifically saving money and energy used for water heating. Here we'll expand on that concept, with a greater emphasis on water conservation. Saving electricity, this chapter's other subject, is presented alongside water conservation because the two are closely related. It takes water to generate electricity, and a great deal of electricity is used in the treatment and distribution of water. See the sidebar on page 130 for more detail on what has been called *the water-energy nexus*.

Throughout the book I try to emphasize the financial payback on green remodeling. That, alone, can be reason enough to make sustainable choices. But we live in a world in which already short supplies of clean water will need to meet the needs of a rapidly growing population. And as the population grows, demand for electricity will expand even faster.

Whether you lie awake nights worrying about the environmental issues that make going green a compelling choice for so many people, or just like to save money, conserving water and electricity makes sense for both reasons.

HOW MUCH WATER DOES IT TAKE TO CHANGE A LIGHTBULB?

It would be difficult, or at least incomplete, to explore water conservation without also talking about reducing electricity use. The two are inexorably linked. Generating electricity consumes vast quantities of water, and an enormous amount of electricity is used for moving and treating water. Four percent of all the electricity generated in the United States is used for the supply, conveyance, and treatment of water and wastewater. That's the national average; in California, the figure is nearly 20%.

Every day billions of gallons of water are consumed by power plants. A single 1,000-megawatt power plant uses 10,000 gallons of water per minute. Much of that water is returned to the sources it was drawn from—but not all of it by any means. And the same water can't be used simultaneously for both power generation and human consumption. In some areas it has become difficult or impossible to obtain permits for new power plants because there is simply not enough water to go around.

Now consider this: Generating the electricity to light a single 60-watt incandescent lightbulb consumes more than a gallon of water per hour of light. Switching to a compact fluorescent bulb will not only reduce the energy used by 60% to 70%, but it will also save several thousand gallons of water per year *per bulb.* So if you are remodeling any part of your house, it makes sense to consider some simple, inexpensive changes to plumbing fixtures and lighting in other rooms as well. It's always nice when you can save money and protect the environment at the same time.

CONSERVING WATER INDOORS

Every day we use water in multiple ways. Showerheads and faucets account for about a third of our indoor water use. Flushing toilets accounts for about 25%. Doing laundry consumes another 20%. Those are the big users. Each category is an opportunity for conserving—without having to sacrifice comfort or cleanliness. We'll take a look at water-saving showerheads, faucets, and toilets in the section that follows. The water savings from efficient appliances will be covered in the section on saving electricity.

Low-flow showerheads

I often think that, for many people, the three scariest words in the English language are "low-flow showerhead." This idea was memorialized in a particularly funny *Seinfeld* episode entitled, appropriately enough, "Low-Flow Showerhead," in which the characters were in a panic because new water-saving showerheads had been installed throughout their apartment building and there wasn't enough water pressure for a decent shower.

The sketchy reputation for water-saving fixtures is not entirely undeserved. When water-saving toilets with a maximum 1.6-gallon flush first became mandatory in the early 1990s, I received any number of irate calls from clients who insisted that my plumber had done something wrong, causing their toilets to clog with some frequency. In reality, the early water-saving toilets just didn't work very well. And the early low-flow showerheads were no better. Fortunately, things have improved.

By now, technology, as it so often does when it's not making things worse, has made things better; new water-saving plumbing fixtures are a huge improvement upon earlier models. Let's start by taking a look at the dreaded low-flow showerhead.

INDOOR WATER USE BY CATEGORY

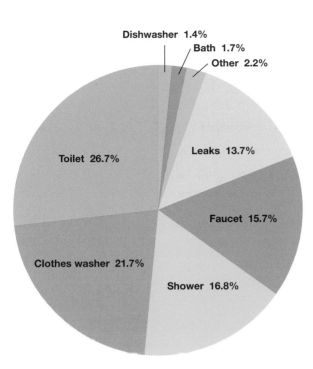

Dishwasher 1.4%
Bath 1.7%
Other 2.2%
Leaks 13.7%
Toilet 26.7%
Faucet 15.7%
Clothes washer 21.7%
Shower 16.8%

Today's low-flow showerheads provide a truly satisfying shower experience while saving both water and energy.

It is not uncommon for older showerheads to use more than 5 gallons of water per minute (gpm)—some of them considerably more. Current federal regulations limit showerheads to 2.5 gpm. Many manufacturers comply by inserting a small plastic flow restrictor. But many homeowners find the water pressure unsatisfactory at this flow rate. And many of them find it surprisingly easy to remove the devices (don't ask me how—I'm not going to tell you), a task that almost anyone can accomplish in about five minutes.

But you can now find relatively inexpensive showerheads with flow rates of 1.85 gpm, or even less, that manage to provide an exceptionally powerful and satisfying output. I installed one in my guest bathroom to try it out, and it is now the most forceful shower in the house.

How do they do it? Borrowing from the same technology used in automobile windshield washers, they control the shape and velocity of water droplets, resulting in a full-body spray that feels like a high-flow shower. The size of the droplets is also optimized to prevent them from cooling off too fast as they travel from the showerhead to your body.

Switching 3.5-gpm showerheads for more efficient new ones can save a family of four as much as 20,000 gallons of water per year, assuming that everyone takes one 8-minute shower per day. (And that's for switching to a 1.85-gpm showerhead; you can easily find quite good showerheads that use as little as 1.2 gpm, so your savings could be greater.) More than two-

WATER AND ENERGY SAVINGS FROM LOW-FLOW SHOWERHEADS

You don't have to deprive yourself of an invigorating shower to save water. One of a new generation of low-flow plumbing fixtures that really work, the Fluidics showerhead from Alsons uses technology developed for automobile windshield washers to control the size and velocity of water droplets, providing a truly satisfying shower with only 1.85 gallons of water per minute.

Gallons per minute for old showerhead	3.50	
Gallons per minute for new showerhead	1.85	
Gallons saved per minute	1.65	
Average length of shower (minutes)	8.00	
Gallons saved per shower	13.20	
Number of people in family	4.00	
Gallons saved per day	52.80	
Gallons saved per year	19,272.00	
U.S. average water cost per gallon	$0.00281	
Water cost savings per year		**$54.15**
Average wastewater charges per gallon	$0.0123	
Wastewater charges avoided		**$236.08**
Hot water saved per year (66%)	12,719.52	
Average cost to heat one gallon of water	$0.03	
Energy cost savings		**$381.59**
Total savings		**$671.82**

thirds of the water used in showers comes from the water heater, so that's about 12,000 fewer gallons of water that need to be heated.

If you look at the cost savings involved, it becomes clear that low-flow showerheads are likely one of the best investments you'll ever make. Assuming an average water cost of $0.0028 (the national average in 2008) and an average energy cost for water heating of $0.03 per gallon, that adds up to a total savings of more than $400. When you add in avoided charges for all the wastewater you didn't send down the drain, the total savings is nearly $700 per year (see the chart above). That's a pretty good return for a couple of $20 showerheads!

Heating 12,000 fewer gallons of hot water also results in a reduction in CO_2 emissions of roughly 2,400 lb., or 1.2 tons. If 10% of U.S. households switched to low-flow showerheads, it would reduce annual CO_2 emissions by roughly 14 million tons. That's the equivalent of taking nearly 3 million cars off the road. It would also save 200 million gallons of potable water per year.

WHY CONSERVE WATER?

You turn on the faucet and water comes out. As much as you want. Whenever you want. Simple, yes? But in many parts of the globe, including the United States, water is growing scarce. Rivers are running dry, lakes are disappearing, and aquifers are becoming dangerously depleted. Across the globe, 1.2 billion people lack access to safe water for drinking, cooking, and bathing. By 2025, the United Nations estimates, this number could swell to more than 5 billion.

In school we were taught that water replenishes itself in a closed cycle. Water in the form of rain and snow falls to earth, feeds rivers and lakes, and seeps through the earth, replenishing groundwater supplies. Plants draw water from the soil and release it into the air through the process of transpiration. The water we consume either filters through the purifying soil into underground streams and aquifers, or it finds its way back to rivers, lakes, and the ocean, then evaporates into the atmosphere and falls back to earth as precipitation. How could we ever run out?

It turns out that not only *can* we run out of fresh water, but we are doing so at an alarming rate. Industrial pollution makes large amounts of water unsuitable for drinking or irrigation, while population growth is outpacing the cycle's ability to replenish itself. Water tables are falling and aquifers are becoming depleted much faster than they can be recharged. And fossil aquifers, such as the vast Ogallala aquifer in the United States as well as others in China and beneath the Saudi peninsula, for example, are not replenishable. When the water in them is gone, it is gone forever.

In the United States, water tables in several grain-producing states have fallen more than 100 ft., and the area that can be fed by rivers in western states is shrinking yearly. The mighty Colorado River, which feeds populations in Colorado, Utah, Arizona, Nevada, and California, is now reduced to a trickle or dries up altogether by the time it reaches the sea. This depletion of rivers and lakes is placing unprecedented strains on ecosystems around the world, leading to the loss of food sources and biodiversity.

As water tables fall, as they are doing on almost every continent, wells for irrigation and domestic water use have to become deeper and deeper, which requires stronger pumps that consume more electricity. In some areas, especially India and China, satisfying the energy demands of increased pumping requires the construction of still more coal-fired power plants. This, in turn, exacerbates air pollution, which degrades water quality, and global warming, which leads to increasing drought in many areas that, in turn, necessitates deeper wells and more pumping. It's a cycle, but not the benevolent, replenishing water cycle we learned about in school.

We can get by quite comfortably with a lot less water than we currently use. For many, it is still a matter of choice. But not for long. For a growing number of us, it is rapidly becoming a matter of dire necessity. This is why conserving water is a prime consideration for any green building or remodeling project.

Nevada's Lake Meade, the reservoir behind Hoover Dam, stood at only 43% of capacity as of May 2009. The band of light-colored rock around the perimeter, bleached from decades of submersion, shows the lake's original level.

Water-efficient plumbing fixtures in this master bath include a 1.6-gpm showerhead, a 0.5-gpm faucet, and a dual-flush toilet. The Richlite® countertops are made from recycled paper and natural resins.

Water-saving faucets

Water-saving faucets produce similar benefits as low-flow showerheads. If you are buying new faucets as part of your remodel, look for the WaterSense label and ask about the faucet's flow rate. The current federally mandated maximum is 2.2 gpm, but there are many faucets on the market that use much less water and still offer satisfactory performance.

If you are not replacing faucets, you can easily and inexpensively replace the existing screw-in aerators that most faucets have. New flow-reducing aerators can cut your faucet's flow rate to 0.5 gpm, an 80% reduction. That could save a family of four more than 12,000 gallons of water per year, in addition to the energy cost savings on the unused hot water. You may find the flow rate of 1 gpm or 1.5 gpm aerators more satisfactory in some bathrooms; they still save a lot of water. Low-flow aerators are also available for kitchen faucets. Retrofitting a low-flow aerator is something anyone can do in about one minute.

▲ The WaterSense label indicates that the fixture meets EPA criteria of being at least 20% more water-efficient than average products of the same type.

◄ New kitchen faucets must meet the federal standard of 2.2 gpm maximum. Older faucets typically use 3 gpm to 7 gpm. If you don't want to replace your faucet, you can save water by installing inexpensive aerators that reduce flow to as little as 1.5 gpm.

Water-saving toilets

The cost-saving potential from water-saving toilets doesn't compare to that of showerheads because toilets only use cold water, but it's not insignificant either. Depending on their age, older toilets use anywhere from 3.4 to 5 gallons per flush (gpf), and some very old ones use as much as 7 gallons. The Energy Policy Act of 1992 limited the allowable amount of water used to flush a toilet to 1.6 gpf.

There's no denying that the early low-flow toilets performed badly. They clogged often and lots of people fell into the habit of flushing twice as a precaution, which pretty much obliterated the expected water savings. There were lots of complaints. Some people actually drove to Canada to bring back 3.5-gpf toilets that were still available there. Eventually, though, most toilets were redesigned to function properly at 1.6 gpf and problems were greatly reduced.

Today, with the need to conserve water becoming more acute, green building standards recommend toilets that use still less water. The Environmental Protection Agency's voluntary WaterSense program provides a label that manufacturers can apply to fixtures that have undergone independent testing to verify they use no more than 1.28 gpf.

There are a few options to choose from when selecting a high-efficiency toilet (HET). There are some single-flush models that meet or exceed the 1.28-gpf standard. Or you can choose a dual-flush model. These have been widely used in Europe for a number of years. Dual-flush toilets generally use 1.6 gallons for a full flush, and 1 gallon or slightly less for a reduced flush. Field studies conducted by the EPA conclude that such toilets average no more than 1.28 gpf in normal use.

The third option is a pressure-assist toilet that uses only 1 gpf. These have been on the market since 2004 and have an excellent track record. They are somewhat noisier to operate, but you'd pretty much have to stuff a shoe in one to get it to clog.

10 EASY WAYS TO SAVE WATER THAT WON'T COST YOU A PENNY

1. Put a few drops of food coloring in your toilet tank to detect toilet leaks. If it colors the water in the bowl, you need to replace the flapper. The U.S. EPA estimates that 20% of all toilets leak up to 200 gallons of water a day, mostly because of faulty flappers.

2. Run the washing machine and dishwasher only when full. This could save you as much as 1,000 gallons per month.

3. Compost food scraps instead of putting them down the garbage disposal.

4. Check your water bill to see if your water usage has increased. That could mean you have a leak.

5. Water your lawn early in the morning to reduce evaporation.

6. Wash produce in a bowl of water instead of under a running faucet. When you're done, use the water in the bowl to water houseplants.

7. Fix leaky faucets; 30 drops per minute wastes more than 1,000 gallons per year.

8. Turn off the water while you brush your teeth (this can save 50 gallons a week).

9. Turn off the water while you shave (this can save more than 100 gallons a week).

10. Cut one minute from your daily shower (this can save 1,000 gallons a year per person).

WAITING FOR HOT WATER

How many minutes of your life have you spent standing outside of your shower, waiting for the water to get hot? If you're like most people, it's a significant number. In many homes it can take from one to three minutes from the time you turn on the shower until the water is warm enough for you to get in. To be conservative, let's call it two minutes. If your showerhead puts out 2.5 gallons per minute and there are four people in your household, this can add up to as much as 7,000 gallons of clean water down the drain every year. Lots of homes have showerheads with much higher flow rates, and in many homes the wait is longer. If we could shorten the wait for hot water, it could prevent the waste of hundreds of millions of gallons of clean water per year.

You would probably be surprised if you added up how much water goes down the drain while you're waiting for it to get hot. Depending on the size of your home and the way it is plumbed, this can add up to thousands, or even tens of thousands, of gallons wasted each year. In some newer homes, the wait for hot water is shortened by a recirculation system. Hot water is pumped continuously through a dedicated plumbing loop, cutting the wait time down to a matter of seconds. But running the pump 18 to 24 hours per day runs up electric bills, and keeping the water in the line hot all day burns energy, too.

Another solution is an on-demand hot water recirculating pump made by Metlund®. When you want hot water, you press a button and the pump begins to circulate hot water through the lines. As hot water begins to flow through the pipes, the cold water it replaces returns to the water heater. When the pipes are filled with hot water, a temperature sensor shuts off the pump. You turn on your shower or faucet and you get hot water without the wait or the waste. You can also activate the pump by installing a motion sensor in your bath-

HOUSEHOLD USES OF WATER

Half of the total water consumption in many homes is used outdoors. Water-efficient landscaping can make a big difference.

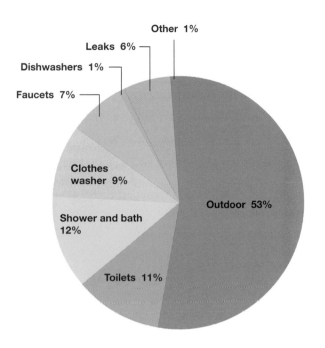

- Other 1%
- Leaks 6%
- Dishwashers 1%
- Faucets 7%
- Clothes washer 9%
- Shower and bath 12%
- Toilets 11%
- Outdoor 53%

An on-demand recirculation pump, installed either under the sink or at the water heater, shortens the wait for hot water, saving thousands of gallons that normally go down the drain every year while we're waiting for it to warm up.

room. When you enter the room, the pump automatically starts up and you don't even have to think about it. If you leave the room for a few minutes and come back, the temperature sensor won't allow the pump to come on again unnecessarily if the water in the line is already hot.

SAVING WATER OUTDOORS

We'll talk about sustainable landscaping in chapter 9, but no discussion of water efficiency would be complete without at least mentioning lawn and garden irrigation. Watering lawns can easily account for 50% or more of a home's annual water consumption. If you happen to be reading this book in the spring or summer and your lawn sprinklers are running, please go shut them off and then turn directly to chapter 9. Otherwise, read on and we'll get to outdoor water-saving ideas shortly.

Water and sustainability

Saving water creates a positive feedback loop. Using less water means less pumping for wells and distribution, which reduces electricity use. The less water we use, the less water needs to be treated, which saves money and energy and can reduce infrastructure needs for the future. And the more slowly we draw down our water resources, the more easily natural cycles can replenish water supplies.

PEX VS. COPPER

In the popular 1987 movie *Moonstruck,* Loretta, the character played by Cher, is the daughter of a plumber, Cosmo Castorini. Cosmo makes a comfortable living replacing the aging pipes in old Brooklyn brownstones. "There are three kinds of pipe," he tells customers in his standard sales pitch. "There's aluminum, which is garbage. There's bronze, which is pretty good, unless something goes wrong. And something always goes wrong. And then," he says, beaming beneficently, "there's copper, which is the only pipe I use. It costs money. It costs money because it saves money."

Today there is another high-quality alternative that can save you money: PEX tubing, though few people had heard of it when *Moonstruck* was released. PEX is short for cross-linked polyethylene. Both flexible and highly durable, PEX tubing can bend around corners so it can be snaked from one end of the house to the other in one piece, saving installation time and eliminating joints and fittings. It is safe for drinking water, and its ability to withstand high temperatures makes it useful in hot-water heating systems. It is especially well suited for radiant-floor heating.

In a typical PEX installation, connections are made at a central manifold, with home runs—dedicated hot and cold water lines—serving each fixture. Hot water delivery is faster because with no joints or elbows to reduce the flow rate, water lines can be narrower, which means there is less cold water to be flushed from the pipe when hot water is called for. This not only adds convenience but also saves water and energy. And because PEX doesn't conduct heat as easily as copper, heat loss is also reduced, saving still more energy.

Some plumbers are still reluctant to abandon copper. Making the switch entails some retraining and special tools need to be purchased, but many now prefer PEX. When it was first introduced, PEX was more expensive than copper, although the convenience and speed of installing it reduced labor costs, leveling out prices. But the dramatic rise in copper prices in recent years has made PEX the more economical choice for most applications today.

I think Cosmo would have approved.

Efficient plumbing design can also reduce water usage and the wait for hot water. The manifold system shown here uses PEX tubing with a home run to each faucet and showerhead.

ELECTRICITY USAGE IN THE HOME

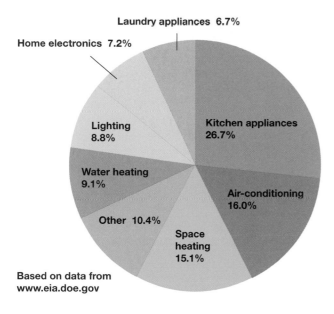

Laundry appliances 6.7%

Home electronics 7.2%

Lighting 8.8%

Kitchen appliances 26.7%

Water heating 9.1%

Air-conditioning 16.0%

Other 10.4%

Space heating 15.1%

Based on data from www.eia.doe.gov

SAVING ELECTRICITY: DON'T FEED THE ELECTRIC COMPANY

Water use is generally confined to a few specific areas, but we use electricity all over our homes. By far, the largest amounts are consumed by heating, air-conditioning, and appliances. We've already talked about reducing energy use for HVAC and water heating in chapter 5, so let's take a look at the rest of the pie.

Refrigerators with bottom freezers consume less electricity than models with the freezer on top.

Appliances

There are plenty of good reasons to consider replacing older appliances as part of a remodeling project—not least of them is saving energy. Together, kitchen appliances and laundry machines consume 33% of the energy used in the average home. Fortunately, today's highest-efficiency appliances consume a lot less electricity than older models. Even appliances not strictly within the ambit of a given remodeling project are worth considering. As long as we're in the appliance store shopping for a new refrigerator, we might as well look at washers and dryers, too. They're just in the next aisle. Such "while we're at it" thoughts often lead to additional up-front costs, but they can also lead to long-term savings.

Refrigerators Your refrigerator is by far the biggest energy hog of any appliance. But big improvements have been made over the years. The amount of electricity you can save with a new, energy-efficient refrigerator depends largely on the age of the one you're replacing. Refrigerators made more than 10 years ago are much less efficient than today's standard models. And 20- or 30-year-old refrigerators that still hum in many American kitchens…one shudders to think about it.

Even among new models there are significant differences in energy consumption. The first thing to do when selecting any appliance is to look for the Energy Star label. Energy Star–qualified

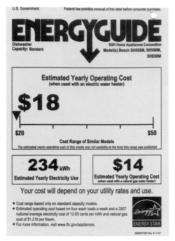

When shopping for appliances, use the EnergyGuide label to compare different brands and models. The label shows how efficient a given appliance is compared with the average for similar units, as well as what you can expect to pay annually for electricity to operate the appliance.

refrigerators use at least 20% less electricity than required by current regulations and 40% less than models made prior to 2001.

The next thing to look at is the yellow EnergyGuide label. This will tell you three things that can help you decide which appliance to buy. The top number is an estimate of the annual operating cost, shown on a scale that tells you how it compares to similar models. The next number tells you the estimated annual electrical use in kilowatt-hours. The estimated operating cost is a function of this and the national average price for electricity. And down near the bottom it tells you what that average is. So if your local utility company charges more or less than the average, you can get an idea of what your actual operating cost will be.

Finally, you'll want to think about the features you want and how they affect the energy use. For example, side-by-side models use more electricity than stacked units, and models with freezers on top use more energy than models with bottom freezers. Conveniences like through-the-door water and ice dispensers can increase a refrigerator's electrical usage by as much as 10%.

Getting rid of the old refrigerator is also a green issue. It is important to dispose them properly because they contain ozone-depleting substances that must be handled safely to prevent environmental damage. Most cities now have appliance-disposal programs, and many retailers and manufacturers have disposal programs, too. Also, your local utility may have rebate or bounty programs for disposal of old appliances, so check with them first.

Doing the laundry

There isn't a tremendous amount of difference in energy use among clothes dryers, which is why they aren't required to carry an EnergyGuide label. But look for a model with a moisture sensor that will turn the dryer off as soon as the clothes are dry. This will cut the dryer's energy use by about 15%.

Washing machines are another story. Energy Star–rated clothes washers not only use less electricity, but if you choose a front-loading model, you'll also use a lot less water and detergent and your clothes will last longer. Another advantage of front-loading washers is that they don't add excess humidity to the air as top-loaders do, so they can improve your indoor air quality while saving you money.

green view

If your kitchen remodel includes the purchase of a new refrigerator, resist the temptation to put the old one in the basement as a spare, as so many people do. (Like me, for example: When I finally replaced the 30-year-old refrigerator that had found its way from my in-laws' pre-remodel kitchen to my basement, I was shocked by how much lower my electric bill was the very next month.) So if you really do need a spare, put the old one out to pasture and get an efficient new Energy Star model. It will pay for itself before you've used up all the leftovers from two or three Thanksgiving dinners.

Lighting

Lighting consumes roughly 15% of the electricity used in a typical home, so it's a good place to find some savings, whether you're remodeling or just upgrading your lightbulbs. By far, the best way to save energy consumed by lighting is to reduce the need for it. In chapter 3 we discussed various ways to enhance the amount of daylight entering your home. The more daylight you have, the less you'll need to turn on the electric lights.

But no matter how much natural light brightens your house during the day, when the sun goes down you need to turn on the lights. Most homes today are still lit primarily by incandescent lightbulbs. But they shouldn't be.

Thank you, Thomas Edison It's fair to say that Edison's invention of the lightbulb in 1879 changed the world. But the continued use of untold billions of the devices is now partly responsible for changing the world in ways Edison could not have foreseen. And not for the better.

The problem is their incredible inefficiency. Only 5% of the electricity consumed by an incandescent bulb produces light; the remaining 95% is emitted as heat. It wouldn't be entirely unfair to say that the modern incandescent lightbulb is essentially a heating device that throws off a little light as a by-product. So not only are we wasting 95% of the electricity we

CFLs are three to four times as efficient as incandescent bulbs and produce 75% less heat.

BUY GREEN POWER

Green remodeling offers many opportunities for reducing your electrical usage. But unless you are able to create a net-zero energy home—not impossible but difficult for most people—you will still be buying electricity to run your lights, appliances, climate-control system, and much else.

Nearly all of the electricity we use in our homes is produced by burning fossil fuels. And more than half comes from burning coal—the dirtiest of all fossil fuels and a major culprit in greenhouse gas emissions.

But you don't have to buy "dirty" electricity. Many utilities around the country now offer green pricing programs. In exchange for a small premium—pennies a day—added to your electric bill, the utility purchases an equivalent amount of energy from a clean power provider. That doesn't mean that the very same electrons produced by, say, a wind turbine will be piped directly to your house; all electrons are the same. But by signing up for a green power program, you will be assured that the *amount* of electricity you use will be generated somewhere from a clean, renewable power source.

If your local utility doesn't offer an option for buying clean energy, you still have choices. For a small fee, you can buy "green tags," also known as renewable energy certificates, which accomplish exactly the same thing. By purchasing green tags, you ensure that the amount of electricity you use will be produced from a clean, renewable, and independently verified source.

Did you know that you can power your home with clean, renewable energy produced by wind, solar, hydroelectric, biomass, or methane captured from landfills and farms?

BUT I DON'T LIKE FLUORESCENT LIGHT . . .

Many people have a negative association with fluorescent lighting, and not without reason. Early fluorescent bulbs tended to produce a cold, bluish light that was both unpleasant and unflattering. But compact fluorescent bulbs that mimic the warm glow of incandescent bulbs are now widely available.

The color of light is measured on the Kelvin scale. Lighting with higher Kelvin temperatures produces cooler light, while lower color temperatures produce warmer light. The warm glow of candlelight has a color temperature of about 1,500°K. Incandescent bulbs produce light in the 2,500°K to 2,900°K range. Older fluorescent bulbs produced a very cool, almost bluish light with a color temperature of about 4,100°K.

Today fluorescent bulbs are available in a variety of shades. Bulbs labeled as "full spectrum" or "daylight" produce light in the 5,000°K to 6,000°K range. When shopping for energy-efficient lighting, look for CFLs with a color temperature of 2,700°K. The light will be virtually indistinguishable from the warm light you get from incandescent bulbs.

▲ Lighting for this green remodel in Minnesota is provided by a combination of low-voltage CFLs and LEDs.

◄ An inexpensive paper shade over a hanging compact fluorescent bulb with a color temperature of 2,700°K casts a warm glow over the dining table of this award-winning green remodel in Texas.

buy to light our homes with, but also our air conditioners have to work harder (burning still more electricity) to remove all that extra heat. And generating all that wasted electricity consumes huge amounts of fossil fuels and contributes to global warming.

Compact fluorescent lightbulbs (CFLs) are three to four times as efficient as incandescent bulbs and produce 75% less heat. So although CFLs are more expensive initially, they save money in the long run. A single CFL will save about $30 in electricity costs over its lifetime at current rates. And the savings continue to add up because CFLs need to be replaced only about one-fifth as often as their incandescent cousins.

But CFLs do present one potential problem—they contain small amounts of mercury. The amount of mercury in a single CFL is minute, but if large numbers of them start turning up in landfills when eventually they do burn out, we could have a problem on our hands.

One solution is recycling. At the end of their useful lives, fluorescent bulbs should be returned to the place where they were purchased or sent to a local recycling facility. You can find the location of recycling plants near you at http://www.lamprecycle.org/ or http://www.epa.gov/bulbrecycling/.

There is another solution on the horizon. Light-emitting diodes (LEDs) are beginning to make inroads into the residential lighting market. Currently used in traffic lights and other commercial applications, residential LED products may soon render other sources of artificial light obsolete. The Department of Energy estimates that over the next 20 years, LED lighting could save $125 billion in electricity costs.

A few good LED products for the home are already on the market. While they are expensive, LEDs can last several times longer than CFLs, use a fraction as much electricity, and contain no mercury. As the technology advances and they become more widely adopted, the cost of LED lighting will certainly come down in the near future. And even at current prices, LEDs can be cost-effective over the long run (see the chart on p.144).

Where to use compact fluorescent bulbs As efficient as they are, CFLs may not be the ideal choice for every lighting need. If you want to consider the most cost-effective options for replacing bulbs, a good rule of thumb is that if a lightbulb is used more than 30 minutes per day, replacing it with a CFL is definitely worth it. But for any lightbulb that is used only a few minutes a day, say, in utility rooms or closets that aren't opened often, it's probably not worth changing it (especially as CFLs take up to a minute to reach full brightness).

CFLs are also not ideal where you need a highly directional light source. Accent lighting for artwork is one example. CFLs give off a more diffuse light, so they're great for ambient lighting. But if there are a few locations where you want to light a small area without a lot of spillover,

DIMMERS SAVE ENERGY AND EXTEND BULB LIFE

Although incandescent bulbs are far from energy efficient, there are some places where they are still more practical than other, more efficient types. Applications that require focused, directional light—spotlights for illuminating artwork, for example—are often best served by incandescent or halogen bulbs. But you can save both money and energy by installing dimmers for those fixtures. Dimmers will not only reduce energy consumption but also will make those bulbs last a lot longer.

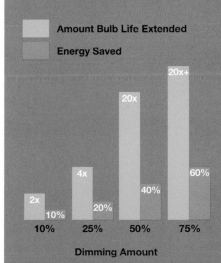

■ Amount Bulb Life Extended
■ Energy Saved

COMPARING LIGHTBULBS

LIFE-CYCLE COSTS FOR THREE TYPES OF LIGHTBULBS WITH EQUIVALENT LIGHT OUTPUT	INCANDESCENT	CFL	LED
Wattage for 800 lumens	60	15	7
Life span of bulbs (in hours)	1,000	10,000	50,000
Cost per lightbulb (in 2009)	$ 0.55	$ 2.98	$ 39.99
Kilowatt-hours of electricity per bulb used in 50,000 hours (@ $0.12 per kWh)	3,000	750	350
Cost of electricity for 50,000 hours (@ $0.12 per kWh)	$360.00	$90.00	$42.00
Number of bulbs consumed in 50,000 hours	50	5	1
Total cost of lightbulbs for 50,000 hours	$ 27.50	$ 14.90	$ 39.99
AMOUNT SPENT ON ELECTRICITY FOR A TYPICAL HOME WITH 30 LIGHT BULBS			
Total annual electricity cost per bulb*	$15.77	$3.94	$1.84
Total annual electricity cost for 30 bulbs	$473.04	$118.26	$55.19
Total electricity cost savings per year		**$354.78**	**$ 417.85**
TOTAL COST OF LIGHTBULBS FOR HOME WITH 30 LIGHTBULBS			
Initial cost of 30 bulbs	$16.50	$89.40	$1,199.70
Number of bulbs consumed in 50,000 hours	50	5	1
Total spent on bulbs over 50,000 hours (approx. 23 years)	$825.00	$447.00	$1,199.70
STRAIGHT LINE PAYBACK FOR PURCHASE OF EFFICIENT BULBS			
Electricity cost per year for 30 bulbs	$473.04	$118.26	$55.19
Annual electricity cost savings		$354.78	$417.85
Amount of time to pay back initial purchase		3 months	2.8 years
AMORTIZED PAYBACK FOR PURCHASE OF EFFICIENT BULBS (20-YEAR LOAN @ 6.5%)			
Additional up-front cost to purchase bulbs		$72.90	$1,183.20
Monthly electricity cost savings		$29.57	$34.82
Monthly interest cost		$0.54	$8.82
Net monthly savings		$29.03	$26.00

* **Assume 6 hours per day**

halogen bulbs may be the best solution. Halogen bulbs are about 20% more efficient than incandescent lamps and contain no mercury.

How many lightbulbs does it take to change a person? Which costs less: a 55-cent lightbulb, a $3 lightbulb, or a $40 lightbulb? The answer seems obvious. But if you compare the life cycle costs—the total cost of devices and electricity over the life of the bulb—for an incandescent bulb, a compact fluorescent lamp, and an LED device, the answer isn't so simple.

If you compare only the initial purchase price, incandescent bulbs win, hands down. But while an average 60-watt lightbulb costs around 55 cents, it uses a lot of electricity and doesn't last very long. A CFL that gives off a comparable amount of light will cost closer to $3, but it uses less electricity and lasts longer. If you have 30 light fixtures in your home, burning incandescent bulbs for six hours a day will cost you about $475 in electricity over the course of a year. Thirty CFLs burned for the same length of time will cost you only about $118 in electricity. The 30 CFLs cost you about $70 more than incandescent bulbs, but the savings on electric bills will make up the cost difference in just a few months.

LED lamps are much more expensive to buy—about $40 compared with that 55-cent incandescent bulb. Thirty of those devices will run you close to $1,200 initially. Ouch! But the pain fades quickly. LEDs use less than half the electricity of CFLs and last five times as long. Over the 50,000-hour life span of one LED, you'll replace a comparable CFL 5 times and an incandescent bulb 50 times. Over the course of 50,000 hours (more than 20 years at 6 hours of illumination per day), incandescent bulbs for 30 fixtures will cost you $825. In that same period, you'd spend $447 for CFLs and $1,200 for 30 LEDs. So for cost of devices, CFLs are the clear winner. But…

If you factor in the cost of electricity, you get still a different answer. Over the course of a year, 30 CFLs will shave more than $350 off your electric bill. If you used LEDs instead, your savings for the year would be a little over $400. At that rate, although CFLs definitely pay for themselves the fastest in just a few months, LEDs will take closer to three years to pay back their initial price premium in electricity savings. That's still a 40% return on investment. And they will continue saving you hundreds of dollars a year for 20 years.

But if you are financing your remodel, as most people do, the picture looks still different. Say you take out a 20-year second mortgage to cover your remodeling costs. If you upgrade from incandescent bulbs to CFLs, your monthly loan payments will be 54 cents higher, while you'll be saving nearly $30 per month on your electric bill. If you upgrade to LEDs instead, it will cost you less than $9 a month in interest to save about $35 per month on electricity.

So, once again, which costs less—a 55-cent lightbulb, a $3 lightbulb, or a $40 lightbulb?

▲▲ **To remove excess humidity after showering or bathing, you should run a bath fan for about 15 minutes. But many people forget to turn the fan off, using electricity needlessly. Controlling the fan with a timer switch solves that problem.**

▲ **Occupancy sensors automatically turn on lights when you enter the room and turn them off several minutes after you exit. For rooms where you only need to turn on the lights after dark, a vacancy sensor must be switched on manually but will automatically turn off the lights once the room is vacant again.**

THE PRIUS EFFECT: HOME ENERGY MONITORS AND CONTROL SYSTEMS

Do you remember when your mother used to say, "Close the door! Don't you know the air-conditioning is on? Are you trying to cool the whole outdoors?" Mothers, it turns out, knew something about energy efficiency. There are a lot of other ways we inadvertently waste energy, and remembering things like shutting off the lights isn't always at the forefront of our thoughts.

Timers and sensor switches

Changing your behavior in small ways (hard, I know) can have a big impact on your utility bills. There are some devices you can install that can help with this. Timers on bath fans and occupancy sensors that shut off the lights in empty rooms are easy, effective, and inexpensive. Of course, these devices don't change your behavior as much as make it irrelevant. Forgot to turn off the lights in the upstairs hall? No matter, they'll turn themselves off.

Timers are great for bath fans. You want to run the fan for 10 to 15 minutes after you get out of the shower to remove excess humidity from the room. But it's easy to forget to turn it off. With a timer, you just set it for the desired amount of time and forget about it with a clear conscience.

For those who have trouble remembering to turn off the lights when leaving a room, there are two types of sensor switches that will do the job for you. Occupancy sensors detect motion or body heat or both and will turn the lights on when you enter a room and turn them off after you leave. These are great for spaces without daylight—storage rooms, laundry rooms, and garages. Many models allow you to program how long you want to wait before they turn out the lights. But in some rooms you don't necessarily want the lights coming on when you enter them during the day. In those areas, what you want is a vacancy sensor. You have to turn the switch on manually when you want the lights on, but the vacancy sensor can tell when you leave the room and turn the lights off for you if you forget.

Home energy monitors

For real behavior modification, you need something that demonstrates the results of your actions. The recent appearance of moderately priced home energy monitors that track and display, in real time, exactly how much energy you are using at any moment makes it easier (and maybe even fun) for you to adjust your energy use patterns.

Studies show that in buildings with energy monitors, energy use goes down 10% to 15%. No arm twisting is involved. No instructions, threats, or ultimatums are necessary. No carrot, no stick: just positive feedback. The effectiveness of energy monitors in reducing energy use is due to a phenomenon that has come to be known as the Prius effect.

Hybrid cars have graphic displays that give a constant readout on fuel efficiency. Drivers of hybrids will often tell you that the visual feedback they get from this motivates them to try to "game the system," so to speak, to improve their gas mileage "score." The ability to see, in real time, the actual effect of their driving habits on the car's fuel efficiency enables them to make small adjustments in their behavior behind the wheel, and the instant visual gratification they see on the screen provides the positive feedback that keeps them at it.

There are a variety of home energy monitors on the market now, ranging from simple, inexpensive devices you can install yourself in a few minutes to sophisticated whole-house systems that monitor all types of energy used in the house. These whole-house monitors even tell you how much you are spending for energy and how much CO_2 your energy use is producing (or saving). Depending on the range of features, home energy monitors run from around $50 to a few hundred dollars.

Optional software packages enable you to record and chart your energy use data on your home computer. Several models can interface with Google™ PowerMeter, a free application that visualizes the information from your energy monitor on a personalized Google homepage. And there are even smart-phone apps that enable you to keep an eye on your home's energy use on the go.

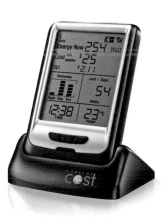

◄◄ The simplest and least expensive energy monitors, such as the Kill A Watt™ EZ, measure the power consumption of one device at a time. You plug your refrigerator or TV into the unit, and it will tell you how much electricity it is using at any given time. These monitors can be useful for finding out what ought to be plugged into a switchable power strip or deciding which appliance you might want to replace with a more energy-efficient model.

◄ Whole-house energy monitors that you can easily install yourself, such as the Current Cost Envi shown here, have wireless displays that can tell you at a glance how much electricity is being used by individual appliances and your entire home at any given moment, by the day, week, or month.

THE ENERGY DETECTIVE

It is often said that you can only manage what you can measure. The TED® (The Energy Detective™) home energy monitor provides real-time household electricity data to enable you to better manage your energy usage. The digital display will show your current energy consumption in kilowatts (kWh) and in dollars and cents per hour. It will also show your projected usage for the day, week, and for the current billing cycle. When connected to a computer running TED Footprints data-logging software, a dashboard displays logged data for up to 13 months, which you can view in the form of graphs, charts, and spreadsheets. It will even show you individual load profiles for all your major appliances. The company's TED 5000 model is designed to interface with Google Power Monitor for remote viewing and analysis.

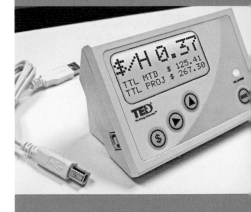

A GREEN CONDO IN MARYLAND

Going green in an apartment presents some obvious limitations; the building's insulation and mechanical systems can't be changed. On the other hand, apartment living can be a lot greener than suburban living. Apartments typically use less energy for heat and cooling; they are usually quite well insulated by other apartments above and below and to either side.

For the owners of this condo in Maryland, moving from a single-family home to an apartment was part of a commitment to downsize their overall environmental footprint. The change also enabled them to transition from two cars to one.

No changes could be made to the HVAC system, but to reduce energy use wherever possible, they installed all new Energy Star-rated appliances and replaced all the incandescent bulbs with compact fluorescent lighting. Home electronics consume a considerable amount of standby power even when switched off. To reduce the energy consumed by these phantom loads, TVs, computers, and stereos are plugged into switchable power strips.

Bringing more natural light into the apartment's interior reduced the need for electric lighting during the day. By removing some walls and cutting openings into others much needed daylight now illuminates a formerly dark kitchen and hallway.

The apartment's original parquet flooring was in poor condition, so it was replaced with sleek, sustainable bamboo. Rather than putting the old flooring in a Dumpster, it was taken to Community Forklift, a supplier of salvaged building materials, where it was later sold to a customer in West Virginia. The vinyl kitchen flooring was replaced with sustainable cork.

This floating desk was fashioned from salvaged lumber by a local artisan.

Many reclaimed and recycled materials were incorporated into the project. Custom-designed light fixtures were forged from recycled metal. Local artisans created a floating desk, bathroom vanity, and a hallway divider of locally salvaged fallen wood. In the kitchen, instead of the usual upper cabinets, the walls are lined with shelves made from salvaged cedar. Reclaimed pine from the rafters of a deconstructed building was used for the pass-through counter, and soapstone for the countertops was found at an abandoned quarry.

In the bathroom, a high-efficiency toilet and a low flow showerhead were installed to conserve water. The bathroom tile, manufactured by American Olean, is made with high recycled content.

▲ Opening up walls and widening doorways bring daylight into the apartment's formerly dark interior.

◄◄ Sustainable features in the remodeled kitchen include Energy Star appliances and shelves made from salvaged wood.

◄ A commitment to craft and sustainability led to the creation of light fixtures forged from recycled metal.

KEEPING COOL, NATURALLY

▶ A whimsical gate, made from recycled steel, leads to an inviting courtyard.

Gail Brager knows ventilation. As professor of architecture at the University of California at Berkeley and associate director of Berkeley's Center for the Built Environment, much of her research is focused on indoor environmental quality, thermal comfort, and the design of naturally ventilated buildings.

So when Gail and her husband, Gino, decided to remodel their home, a modest but nicely detailed 1948 vintage ranch house in Orinda, California, mechanical air-conditioning wasn't even on the table. Gail's general dislike for the feel of artificially conditioned air, coupled with her professional expertise, left no question that this was an opportunity to put into practice many of the principles she teaches every day.

Other important considerations grew out of Gail's design philosophy as well. "The environmental forces of sun, wind, and light," she says, "strongly influence the aesthetic experience of any building, and the consideration of these forces should be a purposeful part of the earliest stages of design." When Arkin Tilt Architects were selected to design the project, it was clear from the start that they had a client whose knowledge and experience would inform the design process in important ways.

PROJECT AT A GLANCE

Originally built: 1948

Original size: 2,765 sq. ft.

Size after remodel: 3,095 sq. ft.

Architect: David Arkin, Arkin Tilt Architects

Contractor: Cal West Builders & Developers

A cupola over the kitchen serves to bring in natural light and draw warm air out. Branches of a Pacific madrone tree, used as a structural column, draw the eye upward.

FOLLOWING THE SUN

Many of the advanced building-science concepts that Gail teaches her students were employed in the remodel. An understanding of thermodynamics and airflow led to strategies that use natural convection currents to dissipate excessive summer heat without any need for fans or air-conditioning. Shading, daylighting, and passive solar design were emphasized using tools such as a physical daylighting model, a pocket sundial, and overlays of fisheye photos and sun-path diagrams. Scale models were set up on site to observe the effects of light and shade on various parts of the structure. Often, models would be modified on the spot with a utility knife to test different configurations.

The need for central heating was also kept to a minimum. Walls and ceilings were insulated with sprayed-in cellulose made from recycled newspaper, and high-R rigid foam board was used on cathedral ceilings to increase R-value and eliminate thermal bridging. Dual-pane windows with low-E coated glass complete the home's efficient thermal envelope. In winter, a Whitfield® wood pellet stove keeps well-insulated living areas warm with very low emissions, reducing the home's total energy use.

The project scope included expanding and remodeling the kitchen, adding a second child's bedroom, and expanding a bathroom. And from beginning to end, the owners' shared commitment to energy efficiency, resource conservation, and indoor environmental quality would inform every decision.

BRINGING THE OUTDOORS IN

One of the Bragers' most important goals was to make the house brighter. The upper part of a dining room wall was removed to increase daylight and allow views of the wooded site. The addition of a shaded south-facing clerestory washes the walls with light, bringing winter sun to the northern parts of the house while preventing overheating from California's intense summer sun.

The courtyard, landscaped with drought-tolerant native plantings, provides comfortable outdoor living space, expanding functionality but not the home's carbon footprint.

▲ A Whitfield pellet stove reduces reliance on the home's heating system. The custom-designed stone mantel absorbs some of the stove's heat and continues radiating it back into the living space after the fire has died down.

▶ Using a locally felled Pacific madrone tree as a column in the light-filled kitchen adds structural support and strengthens a sense of connection to the natural world. Energy Star appliances, bamboo flooring, and low-VOC finishes are among the remodeled kitchen's green elements.

The new kitchen is beautifully daylit thanks to a windowed corner breakfast nook, large north-facing windows, and a glazed cupola. A whimsical touch that serves as a reminder of the home's connection to the natural world is a willowy Pacific madrone tree harvested by the owners and architects. The tree doubles as a structural column for a new beam, while its upper branches reach upward toward the cupola.

Now, the family finds that the formerly dark interior is so bright that they rarely need to turn on the lights during the day. And the enhanced connection to the outdoors visually expands the space and enhances their enjoyment of the home year-round.

✳ Energy efficiency

- Passive solar design enhances ventilation, with careful attention to shading the south-facing glass to keep the house cool in summer without air-conditioning.

- Optimized daylighting strategies reduce the need to turn on lights during the day.

- Fluorescent lighting is energy efficient.

- The refrigerator, dishwasher, and washing machine are Energy Star rated.

- The house uses solar hot water heating.

✳ Resource conservation

- Construction waste was managed through the extensive reuse and recycling of lumber and other deconstructed materials.

- Concrete in the foundation incorporates 35% fly ash.

- Engineered lumber was used for subfloors and sheathing.

- New walls were framed 24 in. on center using FSC-certified lumber. Framing 24 in. on center rather than the usual 16 in. reduces the amount of lumber required to construct walls and increases the amount of insulation by as much as 25%.

- The exterior siding was made from salvaged wood.

- The dining room countertops were made from reclaimed urban redwood.

- Bamboo flooring was placed in the kitchen.

- The bathroom has recycled glass countertops.

✳ Indoor environmental quality

- Low-VOC paint and wood finishes were used.

- A sealed-combustion, direct-vent furnace and water heater were installed.

- The home has improved daylighting and enhanced views of the outdoors.

- Energy Star–rated exhaust fans are in all bathrooms.

A pass-through to the dining room has a countertop made from reclaimed urban redwood with a live edge, a sustainable touch that adds warmth and interest.

7 STICKS AND STONES

What are green homes made of? Will using green building materials in your remodel result in a truly sustainable home? How do you know if a material is truly green? And how green is green enough? In this chapter, we'll look at stuff—the things our homes are made of—and learn what questions to ask about building materials.

There are two principal considerations in determining how green any building material is. The first has to do with the material's impact on the environment. Is it a scarce or endangered resource? Does harvesting or extracting the raw material from the earth cause damage to ecosystems? Does manufacturing—turning the raw material into things we use in our homes—consume excessive energy or create pollution? And how much energy does it take to transport it from its point of origin to your house?

The second consideration has to do with how the material performs once it does reach your house. Does it improve or reduce your home's energy efficiency? Will it hold up over time? And does it contain any chemical compounds that might pose a health risk?

The bottom line, the point of asking these questions about everything that goes into the house, is to learn one thing: Is it sustainable?

▲ Fallen local trees were milled to make cabinets, trim, and baseboards for the green remodel of this 1920s Spanish-style home in Santa Barbara, CA. The legs of the butcher-block island, as well as the range and the granite countertops, were all salvaged or reclaimed.

▶ The striking hardwood floors in this remodeled Victorian in Brookline, Massachusetts, are FSC-certified Brazilian walnut. The FSC label, from the Forestry Stewardship Council, signifies that the wood comes from sustainably managed forests.

WHAT ARE SUSTAINABLE MATERIALS?

Sustainability has been defined as the ability to meet our current needs without compromising the ability of future generations to meet theirs. The whole idea of sustainable materials revolves around the concept of not using up the planet's resources. Some of those resources are tangible—things we can see and touch and use directly, like trees or water, for example. Consuming those resources faster than natural systems can replenish them is not sustainable. Other resources are less tangible but no less important. Our most valuable natural resource, in the broadest sense of the word, is a moderate, benign climate capable of sustaining life. Until recently, this was never something we even thought of as a resource, let alone one that needs protecting. But today it is every bit as endangered as the polar bear.

Direct vs. indirect impacts

What kind of sustainable materials can protect our climate? To answer that, we need to think about direct and indirect impacts. Materials that can directly impact the climate are those with high embodied energy—things that directly cause large amounts of CO_2 to be released into the atmosphere (concrete is a prime example).

Embodied energy, as discussed in previous chapters, is the sum total of all the energy that is expended in producing and using any material, from the energy used to extract the raw materials from the ground to the energy used in manufacturing the material to the energy used in transporting the material from the point of extraction to your house—and even the energy that will be used to dispose of the material at the end of its useful life. Materials with high embodied energy are less sustainable because they are responsible for greater greenhouse gas emissions, which directly impact our climate.

Indirect impacts come from things such as deforestation of tropical rainforests. Tropical woods like mahogany have always been popular because of their rich color and grain and because of their durability. The demand for tropical woods is a significant contributing factor to climate change because rainforests are the lungs of the planet—these vast but dwindling forests absorb huge quantities of carbon dioxide and emit oxygen. Plants, in fact, produce virtually all the oxygen in our atmosphere. Without them, Earth's atmosphere would contain only about 1% oxygen instead of the 20% that keeps us all alive.

Every year the world loses more than 30 million acres of tropical forest—more than the total area of Vermont, New Hampshire, Massachusetts, Rhode Island, Connecticut, New Jersey, and Delaware combined. Excessive logging in most rainforests is illegal, but the laws are extremely difficult to enforce. It has been estimated that 90% of the mahogany imported into the United States comes from illegal logging operations in the rainforests of South America. (Logging is just one of the causes of deforestation. Clearing land to raise cash crops is another.)

We don't need to completely forgo the use of these beautiful woods, but we want to make sure that any tropical woods we do use come from sustainably managed forests (see the sidebar at right).

Can a house be green without using green materials?

Well, yes and no. There are shades of green, ranging from pale green to a deep, rich forest green. But there is no such thing

SUSTAINABLE FORESTRY

Trees grow, we cut them down, and they grow back—right? Well, sort of. But clear-cutting forests and then replanting them with vast tracts of the same species of tree is not sustainable forestry. This results in a loss of wildlife habitat and biodiversity that has extremely negative impacts on the health of the planet.

Sustainable forestry, however, preserves and even enhances the health of forests. Rather than clear-cutting, sustainable forestry involves the careful selection of which trees to cut and which to leave in place so that the natural process of regeneration continues and the soils, watershed, and wildlife habitat remain healthy and productive.

FSC Certification

The Forestry Stewardship Council (FSC) monitors forestry practices and puts its stamp of approval only on lumber that has been harvested in a responsible manner.

Sustainably harvested wood is much easier to find than it was just a few years ago. You can now buy FSC-certified lumber and products made with certified lumber, such as doors, moldings, cabinets, stair parts, and plywood, from retailers including The Home Depot® and many lumberyards. Prices for some items tend to be slightly higher, but the price difference continues to narrow as demand increases. And sometimes it's worth spending a little more to know your remodel is part of the solution, not part of the problem.

The FSC label signifies not only that the wood has come from sustainably managed forests but also that the chain of custody from forest to lumberyard has been documented to prevent substitutions.

When selecting materials for a green home we want to make the most informed and sustainable choices we can. The porch of this home has a floor made of durable, sustainable harvested Ipe.

as a house, or any building, that is absolutely green. Ironically, the greenest thing is no building at all. But unless we want to go back to living in teepees (about as green as you can get), we have to settle for some sort of compromise.

It is possible to make a house extremely energy efficient—even net-zero energy—without using green materials. And it would be hard to argue that a net-zero energy home is not green. But it could be greener still if the materials were chosen for their sustainability.

On the other hand, using the greenest materials in the world won't qualify a house as green if it uses those materials in a wasteful way or if it squanders energy or makes its occupants sick. Ideally, we want to find a reasonable balance between energy efficiency, resource conservation, and indoor environmental quality. And since most of us aren't millionaires, we'll need to make choices along the way about what we can and can't afford. It is easy to make a case for spending money on energy efficiency because that is an investment that will pay for itself. Sustainable materials are also an investment, but the returns aren't as obvious.

We can build a strong argument for investing in the planet's health, but that's often hard to justify when building on a tight budget. Another way to look at it, though, is that as awareness of environmental issues continues to grow, home buyers will be willing to pay more for a house they can feel good about and one that won't expose them to harmful substances and poor indoor air quality. Using green materials might not reduce your monthly utility bills, but it will likely add value to your home.

But do we like it?

Years ago I was the construction manager for a new house in the country, and one of the members of the project team was a famous interior designer who spoke with a thick Eastern European accent. At one of the weekly job meetings, she asked the architect about a certain detail he had designed. He gave her a cogent explanation of his thought process in making this decision, walking her step-by-step through the logic that led up to his ultimate choice. She listened attentively until he was finished. Then, after a longish pause, she looked ever so slightly down her nose at him and said, "Yes, but do ve *like* it?" The clear implication was that *she* did not.

When selecting materials for a green home, we want to make the most informed and sustainable choices we can. But we also want to like the way our choices look. Vitruvius's famous dictum, that a building should embody *utilitas, firmitas,* and *venustas,* could serve as a guide for evaluating materials as well as the whole building. *Utilitas* (utility) refers to function. How well does a material serve the purpose for which it is intended? *Firmitas* (literally firmness, i.e., structural integrity) refers to physical properties, especially strength and durability. How will it hold up? And *venustas* (think Venus, the goddess of beauty) refers to aesthetic qualities. Do we *like* it?

Vitruvius believed that all good buildings must satisfy *each* of these qualities and that each was equally important. What good is a building if it is functional and strong but ugly? What good is a building that is functional and beautiful but doesn't last? And what good is a building that is durable and beautiful but doesn't serve the purpose for which it was intended?

We could ask these same questions about building materials. Vitruvius didn't need to worry about materials that contain toxic compounds, about running out of natural resources because of overpopulation, or about global warming. But we do. The world we live in is much changed since the first century BC. So to his list we must add questions about these things as well (see the sidebar at right).

STARTING FROM THE GROUND UP

Foundations are not generally designed to be seen, so we can dispense momentarily with *venustas.* Of Vitruvius's three qualities, *firmitas* is the critical one here. But unless someone really screws up, it is also pretty much a given that your foundation is going to hold up the house. So if you are building an addition that requires a foundation, what else might you want to ask about?

Concrete is made from abundant materials such as sand, aggregate (crushed stone), and lime, so we don't really need to

green view

In general, here is what you should be asking about each material that goes into remodeling your home.

- Is it made from a scarce or dwindling resource and, if so, what alternatives are available?

- How much embodied energy does it contain, and are there alternatives that contain less?

- Does it contain harmful substances that could put your health at risk?

- Will it perform as intended? *(Utilitas)*

- How long will it last and how much maintenance will it require? *(Firmitas)*

- And finally, do we *like* it? *(Venustas)*

▲ Prefabricated foundation panels, like these made by Superior Walls, use much less concrete than conventional poured foundations. The panels are factory insulated and are made with a high-density concrete that is naturally waterproof, so no chemical waterproofing materials are needed to produce a warm, dry basement.

▲▶ Workers set insulated concrete forms for the addition to a LEED Platinum–rated home in Ann Arbor, Michigan. You can see the completed home on p. 120.

▲▶▶ The average American home consumes two to three acres of forest. Reusing as much of a structure's existing lumber as possible is one way to reduce a remodeled home's environmental impact.

worry about resource depletion. The big issue about foundation materials—that is, concrete—is embodied energy. Concrete contains a lot of embodied energy. Each cubic yard of concrete poured contributes 630 lb. of CO_2 to the atmosphere. If we do the math, it turns out that the greenhouse gas emissions from producing the concrete for one home is roughly equal to the emissions from driving an average car for a year. Considering the number of homes that are built and remodeled each year, you can see how that adds up.

Why does concrete contain so much embodied energy? For one thing, the materials are heavy, so a lot of energy is used in transportation even if the distances are not great. But the real culprit is cement. Many people use the terms *cement* and *concrete* interchangeably, but they are not the same thing. Cement, more correctly called portland cement, is the glue that holds the sand and aggregate together and gives concrete its strength. Ninety-four percent of the embodied energy in concrete comes from producing portland cement. And most of that energy is consumed in heating the raw materials, primarily sand and limestone, to a temperature of 2,700°F and then grinding the result into a fine powder.

A great deal of research is currently being devoted to finding ways to reduce the amount of energy used in cement making, but that could take decades to bear fruit. For the present, the real question for us is simply, how can we use less concrete?

One solution is to substitute fly ash, a waste by-product of coal-burning power plants, for a portion of the cement. Generally, it is possible to make concrete with up to 30% fly ash. This reduces the amount of embodied energy from the production of cement and also makes use of a waste product that would normally be trucked to landfills.

Another way to reduce the amount of concrete is to use engineered precast foundation panels, such as the products made by Superior Wall Systems. These engineered, factory-made foundation panels are constructed much the same as a framed stud wall. The panels get their strength from reinforced concrete ribs and a 1¾-in. concrete "skin" that forms the exterior of the panel. This configuration reduces the amount of concrete used in a foundation by as much as 75%. The company's standard wall system includes 1 in. of rigid foam insulation with an R-value of 5. The company also offers R-12.5 panels with 2½ in. of rigid insulation.

Insulated concrete forms

Another way to make a greener foundation is to use insulated concrete forms (ICFs). Most ICFs are composed of two parallel sheets of rigid foam connected by a web of plastic spacers (they look a lot like big white Legos® made of Styrofoam™). The wall is formed by stacking the hollow blocks, just like Legos, and pouring concrete inside. When the concrete hardens, the forms stay in place and provide a high degree of insulation. While a typical poured concrete wall has an R-value of close to zero, ICF walls can provide insulation values as high as R-27.

Insulated concrete forms don't reduce the amount of concrete in your foundation, but their high insulation value produces substantial energy savings that continue for the life of the house, which more than compensates for the CO_2 emissions resulting from producing the concrete.

HOW GREEN ARE TREES?

Wood is perhaps the most versatile building material on the planet. It is strong, flexible, easily cut and shaped, and plentiful. But the rate at which we construct buildings can outpace nature's ability to replace the trees we cut. The average American home consumes two to three acres of forest, and, as noted previously, we build on average a million new homes per year in the United States. Those homes are primarily constructed of wood. Remodeling often involves sending a lot of that lumber to the dump and replacing it with new lumber from freshly cut trees.

As the population grows, our need for housing continues to rise, which means ever cutting down more trees. So how can the world's forests keep up with that growing demand? There are

green stuff

WHAT IS FLY ASH?

Coal-fired power plants produce more than half of the electricity we consume in the United States today. A by-product of burning that coal is fly ash, which is the noncombustible portion of coal. This fine powder composed of microscopic, glassy spheres is collected from the power plant's exhaust before it can fly away—hence the product's name.

Adding fly ash to concrete is a great example of a win, win, win green building strategy. Power-plant operators save the cost of hauling it to the landfill and instead get paid for material. Concrete made with fly ash is stronger, more workable, and uses less water. And because fly ash replaces up to 30% of the cement in concrete, greenhouse gas emissions are significantly reduced.

The hard, round particles of fly ash have a "ball bearing" effect that allows concrete to be produced using less water. And when mixed with lime, fly ash makes concrete stronger and more durable by filling microscopic voids in the concrete.

Remodeling with one or more types of engineered lumber is one way you can help conserve old-growth forests. Wood I-beams resemble steel I-beams but are made with a web of OSB with top and bottom chords of either sawn lumber or LVL. They enable longer, stronger spans with less wood from virgin trees.

▶ These construction photos from the Ann Arbor project (see p. 120) demonstrate some of the advanced framing techniques that were employed. The roof trusses are aligned with the wall studs, providing adequate load bearing for framing spaced 24 in. on center rather than the standard 16 in. on center

▶▶ A two-stud corner allows insulation to extend all the way to the end of the wall, something not possible with the traditional four-stud corner.

two answers. One is to find ways to build using less lumber. The other is to use lumber that is harvested in a sustainable manner (see the sidebar on p. 161).

Using lumber efficiently

There is not yet enough certified lumber available to meet all our building needs, and the certified lumber that is available is usually a bit more expensive than ordinary wood products. So what other alternatives are there? Again, the answers fall into two categories: engineered lumber and advanced framing techniques. Both have unique advantages, and they are not mutually exclusive—you can employ one or both.

Engineered lumber Engineered lumber comes in many forms but all have one thing in common—they use wood more efficiently than traditional sawn lumber. The first engineered lumber product to gain wide acceptance was plywood. It has been so ubiquitous for so long that we don't usually think of it as engineered lumber, but that's what it is: wood bonded together in one way or another to form something stronger, less expensive, and more versatile than boards of sawn lumber. Plywood in various incarnations has been used off and on for a long time. The earliest examples were discovered by archaeologists in ancient Egyptian tombs. But plywood, as we know it, was developed in the mid 19th century, made possible by the invention of the rotary lathe by Immanuel Nobel (father of Alfred Nobel, who invented dynamite and founded the Nobel Prize). Plywood was first mass-produced during World War II and shortly afterward became a staple of the home-building industry.

Today, engineered lumber takes many forms. Oriented strand board (OSB) comes in 4x8 sheets and is often substituted for plywood in framing houses. Because OSB is made from cross-oriented layers of small strands of wood fiber bonded together by special resins, it doesn't

require cutting veneers from large logs as plywood does. (Many of these resins contain formaldehyde, but formaldehyde-free OSB is now available. However, you have to ask for it—it is still the exception rather than the norm.)

Laminated veneer lumber (LVL) is stronger and more stable than sawn lumber and can be made from fast-growing species like aspen or poplar that are unsuitable for standard lumber. LVLs are available in a range of sizes that can be used as structural beams and substituted for wall studs. While LVL studs are more expensive than the typical 2x4s or 2x6s most homes are framed with, they are perfectly straight and resistant to warping or shrinking. This makes them ideal for use in walls that will support built-in cabinets, where having a reliably straight and true wall makes cabinet installation easier and faster.

Advanced framing techniques Also known as optimized value engineering (OVE), advanced framing essentially means using fewer studs in each wall. Rather than framing walls 16 in. on center, as is typical for most construction, we can place the studs a little farther apart—either 19.2 in. on center (that is, five studs per 4x8 sheet of plywood) or 24 in. on center. In addition to saving lumber, advanced framing offers another advantage. As we noted in chapter 4, wood is a poor insulator, so reducing the amount of lumber in a wall increases the area available for insulation. Advanced framing can improve a home's energy efficiency by 5% to 10% because it allows for more insulation and less thermal bridging.

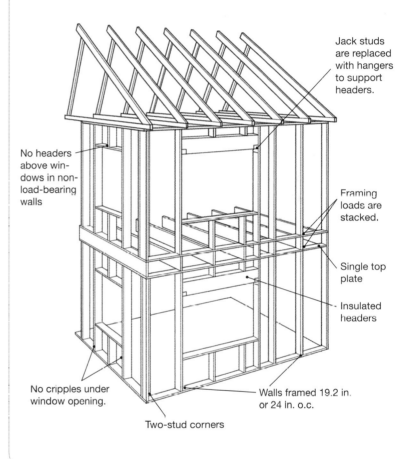

ADVANCED FRAMING
Advanced framing uses lumber more efficiently without sacrificing structural integrity. Every piece of wood eliminated from an exterior wall saves money and allows more room for insulation.

Jack studs are replaced with hangers to support headers.

No headers above windows in non-load-bearing walls

Framing loads are stacked.

Single top plate

Insulated headers

No cripples under window opening.

Two-stud corners

Walls framed 19.2 in. or 24 in. o.c.

Using reclaimed materials

Another way to conserve lumber is to incorporate reclaimed materials into your remodeling project. Every day, thousands of buildings are torn down and large quantities of perfectly usable building materials end up in landfills or incinerators. But there are a number of companies that specialize in reclaiming materials that would otherwise go to waste and return them to the market where they can find new life in other buildings. Doors, cabinets, fireplace mantels, and a host

REDUCING JOB-SITE WASTE

With a little care, you can save money and help the environment by following the most common advice in any discussion of green building or remodeling: reduce, reuse, and recycle.

REDUCE: ORDER CAREFULLY

- When possible, order lumber in precut lengths. Cutting on site often results in trash bins filled with short pieces of expensive materials.
- When ordering flooring and other decorative materials, ask your installer how much to figure for waste. We often have a tendency to guess on the high side.
- Use materials efficiently. Consider framing 24 in. on center rather than the usual 16 in. You'll save lumber and make more room for insulation.

REUSE: DECONSTRUCT OR DEMOLISH?

- If you are taking down part of a structure, deconstruct it. In many cases, you can reuse a lot of the old lumber, as well as items like doors, trim, and hardwood flooring. You'll save the cost of new materials and the cost of hauling away the old.
- Look for a salvage company that takes cabinets, countertops, appliances, and plumbing fixtures for later resale. In some cases, you can even get a tax deduction for donating reusable materials.
- Consider buying some items at a salvage yard. Often you can find beautiful, well-made things at reasonable prices. Someone else's waste might be your treasure.

RECYCLE: SEPARATE OR COMMINGLE?

- Many waste-management companies now routinely separate recyclable materials at a sorting facility. If you can find a hauler that does, you can put everything in the same trash bin. But ask them if there are any items they cannot accept in mixed loads.
- If your hauler doesn't separate, sort out recyclables as waste is generated and place them in separate containers. Common job-site waste materials that can be recycled are cardboard, gypsum wallboard (drywall), glass, and metal.

The walls of this old structure in Cambridge, MA were carefully deconstructed. Nearly all the old lumber was reused, reducing the amount of new materials required. The completed green remodel can be seen on page 106.

of other excellent finds are now turning up in many remodeled homes, adding character, conserving resources, and often providing economical substitutes for new materials.

Flooring is one area where there is a particularly rich trove of reclaimed materials that are readily available for purchase. Some of it comes from old industrial buildings, some from barns, and some from logs that have been submerged underwater for decades—logs that sank while being transported downstream to sawmills, for example. Reclaimed flooring is typically more expensive than virgin material, but it adds a rich patina that only age can produce and can be found in a wide selection of beautiful woods, many of them no longer available from new sources.

What is the difference between reclaimed and recycled? The terms *reclaimed* and *recycled* are sometimes used interchangeably, but they are not exactly the same thing. In general, reclaimed materials are those that are salvaged from the waste stream and put back into service in essentially

▲ Reclaimed flooring such as these antique American chestnut planks can add beauty and character while conserving natural resources.

◄◄ Reclaimed structural beams from an old theater were put to two different uses in this green remodel. For the floating stair treads, the reclaimed wood was shaped and sanded to a smooth finish. For the legs of a custom dining table, the beams were cut to length but otherwise left unchanged.

Recycled-glass tiles line the shower of this green bathroom remodel. The countertop is Richlite, made from recycled paper pulp and natural resins.

the same form as their original use—that is, boards of one type are reused as boards of another type. Barn beams sawn into flooring are one example.

Recycled materials are those that have been salvaged but then reprocessed or reconstituted into other forms. Some recycled materials are 100% recycled, such as steel beams made from melted-down cars or recycled glass tile made from old bottles, for example. Others contain varying amounts of recycled content. But they still keep a lot of perfectly usable raw materials out of landfills.

Countertop choices

One of the most important choices for any kitchen remodel is the countertop material. Naturally, you want it to look great because it is so prominently visible. But when you're doing a green kitchen remodel, you also want it to be sustainable; the same questions you'd ask about any other material still apply (see the sidebar on p. 163).

There are many good countertop choices for green kitchen and bathroom remodels. Here's a quick look at a few of the more popular ones.

Stone Natural stone countertops, such as granite, marble, and slate, are good looking and extremely durable. Stone is not a diminishing resource, but it has a lot of embodied energy because it is heavy; transporting it uses a lot of energy and quarrying it causes considerable environmental damage. Choosing stone that is quarried within a 500-mile radius reduces embodied energy. If you can find a reclaimed stone countertop, so much the better. Most require treatment with a sealer to make them stain resistant, so you want to make sure to use a nontoxic product.

Plastic laminates and solid-surface countertops The main green issue with these countertops is with the substrate and adhesives. Ask for a formaldehyde-free substrate material and low-emitting adhesives.

Paper/resin slabs PaperStone™ slabs, made from recycled paper and resin, are hard, durable, and impervious, and are no more prone to scratching than natural stone countertops. They come in solid or slightly mottled colors and often resemble soapstone. Another similar product from Richlite is made from wood fibers, waste paper, or corrugated cardboard, but you'd never know that from looking at it. Both of these products are manufactured on the West Coast, so keep in mind that the farther they are shipped the more embodied energy they contain.

Wood Because of its warmth, wood is a popular countertop choice for many homeowners. Selecting lumber from sustainably managed forests or reclaiming it from prior uses are environmentally friendly choices.

Concrete Concrete is a highly durable countertop choice that can be cast in many forms, colors, and finishes. Adding recycled content such as fly ash helps reduce the material's high embodied energy.

Recycled glass Solid glass countertops are made from recycled glass, melted down and cast into luminous slabs of various colors. Different brands contain varying amounts of recycled material, so look for the highest percentage of recycled content. Some, like Bio-Glass™, are made from 100% recycled glass.

▲▲◄ **Reclaimed lumber from a nearby home damaged by Hurricane Katrina found new life as shelves and countertops in the green remodel of a New Orleans shotgun cottage.**

▲▲► **Squawk Mountain Stone countertops are composed of recycled paper, recycled glass, coal fly ash, and cement. The material is hand-cast into slabs that resemble soapstone or limestone.**

▲◄ **Recycled glass and concrete make up this terrazzo countertop.**

▲► **This translucent countertop material from Bio-Glass is made from 100% recycled glass.**

COOKING WITH SUSTAINABLE MATERIALS

When Amy and Oscar decided to remodel 600 sq. ft. of their 950-sq.-ft. Manhattan apartment, green wasn't on their wish list. But it was high on the wish list of their architect, David Bergman. The clients wanted lots of color, a fabulous open kitchen, and a home office. They didn't want to pay a premium for something they weren't looking for in the first place, they told him, but as long as they liked the look and could afford it, they were willing to go along.

David showed them various material choices without telling them which ones were environmentally friendly. More often than not, he said, they liked the green materials. The result is a colorful, comfortable home with cork floors, locally sourced recycled-glass countertops, recycled-glass tile backsplashes, and cabinets made of wheatboard with FSC-certified veneers. In the home office, the desktops are natural linoleum.

To make the most of limited space, a constant challenge in New York apartments, a windowless galley kitchen and a tiny spare bedroom were combined, creating an airy, loftlike space that incorporates living and office areas, and allowing borrowed natural light to brighten up the entire space—another green bonus. Moveable recycled-content resin panels hide both the utility closet near the kitchen and the file cabinet in the office, adding flexibility.

▲▲ An integral part of this Manhattan apartment's open living, working, and eating space is a showcase of sustainable materials including rapidly renewable cork floors, wheatboard cabinets with FSC-certified veneers, and sliding panels of recycled-content EcoResin.

▲ The open plan allows daylight to illuminate the home office and a formerly dark kitchen. The desktops are natural linoleum, made from wood flour and vegetable oils. Low-VOC paints, finishes, and adhesives were used throughout.

◄ A backsplash of recycled-glass tile perfectly complements the recycled-glass countertop, locally sourced from IceStone in Brooklyn, New York. The cabinet knobs are also recycled glass.

Terrazzo-type countertops, such as IceStone®, are made from chips of recycled glass embedded in cement and polished to a smooth surface full of shiny flecks. The product comes in a wide range of colors. Most brands contain 85% to 100% recycled glass.

Rapidly renewable materials

Yet another way to reduce the strain on the planet's resources is to use materials that regenerate quickly. Fast growing bamboo can substitute for oak flooring from 80-year-old trees. Technically a grass, bamboo grows to full height in less than five years and can be harvested over and over.

Cork comes from the bark of the cork oak tree. It can be harvested dozens of times over the tree's 200-year lifespan. Most cork flooring is made of scraps from the production of wine bottle stoppers, which qualifies it as both rapidly renewable and recycled.

Kirei board is made from an agricultural waste product, sorghum stalks, which are normally burned or placed in landfills. Wheatboard, another material made from farm waste, is a lightweight, formaldehyde-free alternative to particleboard and can be used in making cabinets, furniture and flooring.

Selecting sustainable materials is a great way to eliminate waste. It makes efficient use of natural resources and gives new life to previously used materials that would otherwise end up in the dump. We'll continue discussing materials in the next chapter, where we'll look at them from the point of view of how they affect our health and the air we breathe inside our homes.

There are two possible issues that should be considered in choosing bamboo for your home. One is that virtually all the bamboo on the market is made in China. This means shipping the finished product long distances. Whether the embodied energy content of bamboo flooring outweighs the environmental benefits of preserving old-growth hardwood trees is probably impossible to know with absolute certainty. My opinion is that saving trees tips the scales in bamboo's favor.

The other concern with bamboo is whether the binders that hold it together contain formaldehyde. Most of the bamboo available for purchase here comes from reputable sources that document what's in their products. But you should always ask to see product data sheets when buying bamboo to make sure you know what you are getting.

▼ ◄ ◄ **Bamboo flooring goes down just like hardwood flooring.**

▼ ◄ **Cork has been used as flooring since the 19th century.**

▼ **Kirei board, used for furniture, countertops, and other applications, is made from agricultural waste (sorghum stalks), which gives it its unique grain pattern.**

FOURSQUARE AND GREEN

The 1970s kitchen of this 1904 foursquare house in Seattle was in serious need of updating and many building systems had to be modernized, but the owners wanted to retain the home's original character. For their green remodel, they chose to use as many recycled and reclaimed materials as they could, especially those that were locally sourced.

Improvements to the building envelope included recycled denim insulation, careful air sealing, and double-glazed, low-e, argon-filled wood windows to replace the old single-glazed aluminum windows. This enabled them to replace the old furnace and hot water heater with a single high-efficiency hot water heater that supplies wall-mounted European-style radiators with heat for the entire house.

Interior walls were removed to open up the kitchen to the dining room. The lumber was salvaged for use elsewhere in the house and the leftover doors were reused in the basement. A chimney running through the center of the house was removed—the new high-efficiency replacement doesn't require one—and the bricks were saved for later use.

The kitchen flooring is the original fir, restored after being buried under layers of vinyl and linoleum, with additional reclaimed fir purchased from the ReStore, a local nonprofit building-supply company. After sanding, the floors were finished with natural Osmo Polyx® oil. Choosing cabinets from IKEA® allowed the owners to spend money on quality appliances—Energy Star, of course—and to use locally sourced PaperStone countertops, made from 100% recycled paper with cashew oil and resin for bonding.

Reclaimed fir flooring and countertops made from recycled paper are just two examples among a host of green features packed into this green remodel in Seattle.

HOUSE ON GRANDFATHER MOUNTAIN

Sometimes a house just waits for the right buyer to come along. When Martha and Robert discovered the house at Grandfather Mountain, near Boone, North Carolina, it had been languishing on the market for three years. Area realtors considered the house a teardown. But looking at the property, Martha wasn't so sure about that. To her it seemed as though it had possibilities. She wanted a second opinion, so she called architect Don Duffy and asked him to have a look. He agreed with Martha's take on the house.

Not tearing down a house is almost always greener than starting over; it's the one thing that all green renovations have in common. Remodeling, as we have seen, gives new life to large amounts of all sorts of materials, thereby reducing the waste stream that ends up in landfills and limiting the demand for virgin materials that must be harvested or extracted from the earth. It also saves the energy normally consumed by extracting, processing, and shipping those materials.

PROJECT AT A GLANCE

Originally built: 1973

Original size: 2,605 sq. ft.

Size after remodel: 3,285 sq. ft.

Architect: Don Duffy Architects

Location: Boone, North Carolina

Envisioning possibilities in an overlooked property saved this house from the wrecker's ball. Interior space was reorganized and expanded with only minor additions to the foundation. Thoughtfully placed doorways and windows admit ample daylight and promote good cross-ventilation.

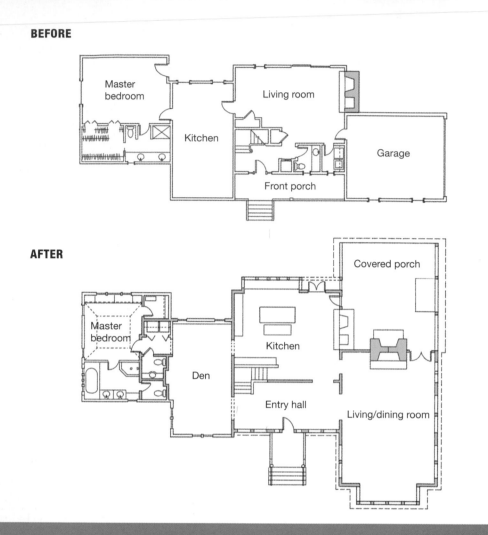

BEFORE

AFTER

CREATING SPACE

Staying small is another green strategy the clients and architect embraced. To provide the added functionality the owners desired, an attached two-car garage to the right of the front door was recaptured as living space and became the new living/dining room. The roofline over this space was reconfigured and extended toward the rear, covering part of the terrace to create an outdoor room. An exterior fireplace that shares a chimney with one just behind it in the living room makes the space usable in all but the coldest months of the year. Outdoor living space is a great way to make a home live larger without greatly enlarging its carbon footprint.

For the enclosed space, energy efficiency was boosted by the addition of new insulation, double-pane windows, careful air sealing and weatherstripping, and a high-efficiency propane furnace. Energy Star appliances and energy-efficient lighting also do their part to keep electrical usage down.

▲ This rustic home in North Carolina's Blue Ridge Mountains was remodeled using a sustainable palette of natural, locally sourced, and recycled materials.

◄ A spacious outdoor room adds valuable living space without adding to the home's energy usage. A wood-burning fireplace makes the space comfortable and inviting in all but the coldest months.

▲ Accents of artfully laid stone suggest both simplicity and refinement. Sourcing the material from the surrounding hills kept embodied energy low.

▶ Cradle to Cradle–certified Bark House shingles, made from the bark of locally sourced poplar trees (which is normally a waste product), add an Arcadian flavor that seems ideally suited to the mountainside location.

LOCAL MATERIALS

But where this house really shines is in its extensive use of natural, reclaimed, and locally sourced materials. With vision and creativity, the architect and clients incorporated materials with the least environmental impact.

The siding is made from the bark of poplar trees, which is normally discarded by lumber mills or turned into mulch. Locally sourced, this reclaimed material, marketed under the name Bark House® siding, is produced just 50 miles away. Its manufacturer, Highland Craftsmen Inc.®, in Spruce Pine, North Carolina, collects all the bark it uses from within a 100-mile radius of its facility. For their very low embodied energy, diversion of materials from the waste stream, durability (life expectancy is 75 years or more), and recyclability, these shingles carry the highly regarded Cradle to Cradle certification at the Gold level.

Logs of locally harvested locust trees were used with minimal processing for the porch columns and railings. Locally quarried stone is another important element in the all-natural palette of materials selected for both interior and exterior use.

Inside the house, twigs and branches from the forest floor add picturesque character to the stair railing. Interior walls of unfinished pine complement the home's rustic flavor and will never need painting, which further reduces the home's environmental footprint.

❋ Extensive use of reclaimed and locally sourced materials diverts material from landfills and keeps embodied energy low.

❋ Substantially increased living space with only minor expansion of the home's footprint provides added functionality with minimal need for new building materials.

❋ Aligning doors and windows admits more daylight and promotes natural ventilation.

❋ A generous covered porch with fireplace provides additional living space for much of the year without consuming energy for heat or air-conditioning.

▲ Much of the interior detailing is left un-finished, adding to the all-natural look and reducing maintenance as well as environmental impacts associated with manufacturing paint.

◀ Aligning doors and windows visually expands interior space and promotes good cross-ventilation, which reduces the need for air-conditioning.

8

BREATHE EASY:
CREATING A HEALTHY LIVING ENVIRONMENT

We spend a lot of time in our homes. If you are like most people, you think of your home as an oasis, a safe haven, a sanctuary from the busy, dirty, and occasionally inclement world outside our doors.

You look to your home for protection—protection from extreme heat and cold, wind, rain, snow, hail, sleet, and a whole variety of things, animate and inanimate, that might intrude on your family's well-being.

But what about your health? Can your home protect you from getting sick? Or does it expose you to potentially harmful substances? Previous chapters have considered ways in which homes can protect the health of the environment. In this chapter we'll take a look at what green remodeling can do for the health of you and your family.

Energy efficiency wasn't on anyone's mind when older homes, like this Connecticut farmhouse, were built. There was little effective insulation and construction was anything but airtight, but the amount of fresh air that leaked in was more than enough to prevent indoor air-quality problems.

IS YOUR HOUSE MAKING YOU SICK?

Americans spend, on average, 90% of their time indoors. For young children and the elderly that number is even higher. Yet the air in many homes has far higher levels of pollutants than outdoor air. This is a relatively new phenomenon. Fifty years ago, the indoor air quality of American homes was far healthier than it is today. When did that change, and why? We can look to two major causes of worsening indoor air quality, both of which can be dated with some precision.

Prior to the middle of the 20th century, there were few, if any, synthetic materials used in home construction. Granted, those homes weren't insulated particularly well, but that, as it turns out in at least one regard, was a blessing as well as a curse. They required a whole lot of energy to keep warm, but energy was cheap and we were still blithely unaware of the environmental problems caused by the burning of fossil fuels.

On the plus side, there was plenty of fresh air—homes were so leaky that any pollutants that did find their way into the house were quickly vented to the outdoors. It was not uncommon for homes to go through eight or nine complete air changes per hour. (This is still the case for millions of American homes—something that desperately needs to be addressed.)

A major push for improved insulation occurred in the early 1970s when the steep spike in energy prices caused by the 1973 OPEC oil embargo made conservation an instant national priority. Building codes were quickly revised to require that homes, as well as commercial buildings, were constructed with a lot more attention to keeping the warm air inside. As insulation standards increased, air infiltration was reduced. While this saved energy, there were unintended consequences that resulted in a whole new set of problems that many of us live with to this day. That was one cause.

The other was that this trend toward tighter construction followed close on the heels of a revolution in building materials. What was that revolution? It could almost be summed up in one word—as it was in a memorable scene from the 1967 film *The Graduate.* "I want to say one word to you," the recent grad played by Dustin Hoffman was advised. "Just one word. Plastics."

Of course, it's more than just plastics. In fact, many plastics are quite benign. But it's convenient shorthand for a revolution in the way we made just about everything. This revolution was neatly summed up by a famous advertising slogan of that era, "Better Things for Better Living . . . Through Chemistry." We were modern now and everything was going to be different. Our homes and everything in them were suddenly being made from materials not found in nature.

Alphabet soup

Better living through chemistry created an alphabet soup of new compounds, some of them potentially toxic, like VOCs (volatile organic compounds), SVOCs (semivolatile organic compounds), HFRs (halogenated flame retardants), and PFCs (perfluorochemicals), that found their way into commonly used

CHOOSING NONTOXIC MATERIALS

Many of the materials commonly used in homes today contain potentially dangerous chemicals that are known or suspected to have adverse health effects. In general, any material with a noticeable odor is likely to contain harmful substances. But just because you can't smell something doesn't necessarily mean it is safe. Here are a few tips for choosing safer alternatives:

- Use low-VOC or zero-VOC paints, stains, and floor finishes.
- Select carpeting and rugs that carry the Green Label Plus certification from the Carpet & Rug Institute.
- Carpeting should be installed over low-VOC, formaldehyde-free padding without brominated flame retardants.
- Ask to have your carpet and padding unrolled in the warehouse to air out for at least 24 hours before delivery.
- Avoid vinyl flooring and wall coverings, which are high in phthalate plasticizers. Cork and linoleum are nontoxic alternatives.
- Use low-VOC adhesives for wall coverings and flooring.
- Choose cabinets and furniture made from formaldehyde-free plywood or particleboard.
- Avoid wrinkle-resistant fabrics—most are treated with formaldehyde.
- Use green cleaning products.

Two healthy choices in one kitchen. Linoleum, made from renewable materials such as wood flour, linseed oil, and pine rosin on a jute or burlap backing, is a healthy, sustainable, and durable flooring choice that comes in a wide array of colors and patterns. The bamboo cabinets are made with a formaldehyde-free soy-based adhesive and a low-VOC finish.

IS YOUR SHOWER CURTAIN MAKING YOU SICK?

We're all familiar with the pungent smell of a new vinyl shower curtain. What we're smelling is a category of chemicals called phthalate plasticizers, which give vinyl and other plastics their flexibility. Phthalate plasticizers, which are also contained in PVC and a variety of other synthetic materials, have been linked to bronchial irritation, asthma, and liver damage, as well as potential damage to the reproductive, respiratory, and endocrine systems.

Keeping water off the bathroom floor is important, but must we poison ourselves in the process? Fortunately, you have several choices. Shower curtains made of PEVA, a nonvinyl, nonchlorine-based plastic, are inexpensive and easy to find in a wide range of colors and patterns. Another choice is to use a cotton or polyester shower curtain liner by itself—also easy and economical. (Polyester, counterintuitively, may be a more ecologically friendly choice than cotton because growing cotton requires large amounts of water and pesticides.) At the other end of the price spectrum, glass shower doors are available for bathtubs as well as shower stalls, and are nontoxic, long lasting, and easy to keep clean.

building materials such as paints, adhesives, wood finishes, furniture, fabrics, floor and wall coverings, appliances, cleaning supplies, and more.

Not everyone is equally sensitive to every chemical, and lots of people do not experience acute or severe symptoms. For many, living with chemicals does trigger harmful effects in the short term. For all of us, though, long-term exposure to certain chemical compounds carries the potential for a variety of health risks, some of them serious. Remodeling is generally thought of as home improvement, but how much of an improvement is it if we inadvertently expose our family to hazardous substances?

VOCs, found in many building materials, especially paint, wood finishes, and adhesives, are carbon-based chemical compounds that can evaporate at normal room temperatures in a process known as off-gassing. Over time they mix with the air we breathe in our homes and offices. VOCs such as formaldehyde, acetaldehyde, toluene, and benzene have been associated with a range of symptoms including dizziness, headaches, and eye, nose, and throat irritation. In some cases, they may also cause damage to the liver, kidneys, and nervous system, as well as increase the risk of certain types of cancer.

SVOCs are commonly found in materials such as vinyl wallpaper, foam carpet padding, upholstered furniture made with polyurethane foam, and carpeting that's been treated with pesticides as well as fabrics treated with halogenated flame retardants. SVOCs are increasingly showing up in human milk, blood, and tissue samples, raising serious concerns about their long-term health risks, even at low concentrations. Many products continue to release SVOCs long after they have stopped out-gassing VOCs.

We don't even know the effects of most of the substances we come in contact with inside our homes. Consumer products contain thousands of chemical compounds; only a tiny fraction of them have ever been tested for toxicity to humans. Of the 80,000 chemicals used in manufacturing, the U.S. Environmental Protection Agency has identified 16,000 as "chemicals of concern." But only about 250 of them have ever been tested for their effects on humans.

And even the ones that *have* been tested are tested only for exposure to high concentrations over a short period. Among scientists today there is a growing consensus that long-term exposure to very small concentrations of certain chemical compounds may pose significant risks to our health.

It's not just chemicals

Chemicals aren't the only cause of potentially harmful indoor air quality. Garden-variety irritants like dust and pollen blow in through open doors and windows and are tracked in on our shoes,

Fiberglass furnace filters are designed to protect the furnace, not your lungs. They can stop particles large enough to damage the innards of the furnace, but for protecting your innards you want a high-efficiency pleated filter with a MERV 8 rating or higher.

WHAT IS OFF-GASSING?

Off-gassing is the evaporation of volatile compounds into the air. Some materials, like paint and adhesives, release most of their volatile chemicals rather quickly and then taper off. Others, such as products containing vinyl or polyurethane foam or fabrics treated with flame retardants, continue off-gassing substances into the air for much longer periods. According to a paper published by the Healthy Building Network, VOCs, especially in wet-applied products like paints, finishes, and adhesives, are emitted at high levels when a product is first installed and taper off to lower levels as time goes on, although temperature and humidity changes may increase them again.

VOC emissions from solid materials, such as flooring and furniture, continue over longer periods of time. And SVOCs are released much more slowly at first, but some products actually emit more SVOCs at later points in their life cycle than they do in the beginning.

as are pesticides from our lawns. Mold spores, which are found everywhere, can start to grow on damp surfaces. Pet dander from the family dog or cat can cause allergic reactions in some people. Dust mites, another common allergen, collect in carpet, upholstery, and bedding and multiply even faster in humid conditions.

So what are we to do with all this information? Holding your breath is a short-term solution at best. I don't recommend it. Fortunately, more practical alternatives are at hand, and remodeling is a good time to do something about it.

THREE STEPS TOWARD A HEALTHIER HOME

The standard mantra for good indoor air quality (IAQ) is "elimination, ventilation, and filtration." Any pollutant we can eliminate before it enters our air supply is one less thing to worry about. Choosing materials with care is one way we can accomplish that. Many pollutants are also introduced through human activity—smoking is a prime example. But cooking, pets, hobbies, and simply walking into the house with our shoes on are all potential culprits.

Proper ventilation is also crucial for healthy IAQ. A great deal of indoor air pollution is generated by humans, and a lot of that is simply unavoidable. So fresh air supplied at a controlled rate is essential. Whole-house ventilation was covered in chapter 4, but we will touch on it briefly in this chapter, particularly as it relates to air quality.

Airborne pollutants we fail to eliminate through source control or ventilation can be removed through air filtration. We'll go into more detail about air filters at the end of this chapter. For now, suffice it to say that the fiberglass filters that come with most furnaces—especially older ones—are essentially useless for stopping anything small enough to be inhaled. To remove smaller particles requires at minimum the use of high-efficiency pleated filters on your air system.

ELIMINATE POLLUTANTS AT THE SOURCE

Eliminating the source of indoor air pollutants is, perhaps, the most effective means of achieving healthy indoor air quality—anything that can be prevented from intruding into our homes in the first place doesn't need to be gotten rid of. Pollutant source control is our first and best line of defense. It can be accomplished in three important ways.

RAIN SCREEN SIDING

Rain screen siding minimizes the risk of water intrusion by creating a drainage plane that allows moisture to drain and an air space that enables the back of the siding to dry out. This detail can be executed using felt paper or house wrap, but specialized rain screen materials provide a higher level of protection while still allowing the wall to breathe.

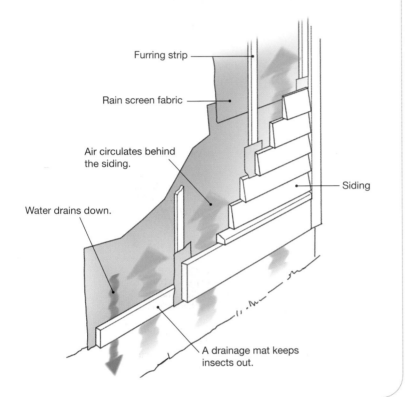

Furring strip

Rain screen fabric

Air circulates behind the siding.

Siding

Water drains down.

A drainage mat keeps insects out.

green view

In most remodeling projects, it isn't practical to expose existing foundation walls to add insulation. But you can insulate cold water pipes, another common place for condensation to form. Insulating cold water pipes is easy and inexpensive, and it's something you can probably do yourself with foam pipe insulation found at most hardware stores.

Moisture and humidity control

Mold and bacteria love a humid environment. Damp basements, humid bathrooms, and laundry rooms are among their favorite places to be fruitful and multiply. Construction details that prevent moisture from entering the home are an essential part of every remodeling project, but it's surprising how often some detail is overlooked.

Roof overhangs, window casing with projecting crown heads, porticos, and the like all play a role in keeping rain from beating against the most vulnerable parts of the house. Properly flashed connections, at windows, doors, and where roof planes meet, are also essential. Most people don't realize that house siding is not impermeable. Some water always finds its way past this first line of defense, so providing a drainage plane between the siding and the sheathing is necessary to complete your home's raincoat (see the drawing at left).

Basements are notoriously damp places, but they don't have to be. We can direct water away from the foundation and prevent condensation on interior surfaces. Correctly installed footing drains, gutters, and downspouts that direct rainwater away from the foundation, as well as proper grading of the soil around the house, all work together to prevent the intrusion of bulk water. Ideally, the ground should be graded so that it slopes away from the house for a minimum of 3 ft. around the entire perimeter.

Condensation occurs when the surface temperature of any material is below the dew point of the air. The more humidity there is in the air, the higher the dew point. Think of your foundation as a glass of iced tea. The glass is cold and the summer air is humid, so condensation forms quickly. To prevent condensation, we can either reduce the humidity or raise the surface temperature—or preferably both. Condensation doesn't appear on a glass of water that is at room tempera-

ture. If you can insulate your foundation from the outside, the interior surface will become closer to room temperature so condensation won't form.

Your next line of defense against moisture is reducing indoor humidity levels. This is best accomplished by using bath fans and kitchen vent hoods to remove water vapor in the areas of highest concentration. Bathroom exhaust fans vented to the outside are highly effective in removing unwanted humidity. Look for fans with the Energy Star label to keep energy costs down. I also recommend controlling bathroom fans with a timer switch (see p. 146). You want the fan to run for 10 to 15 minutes after bathing or showering. But if you're like me, you'll probably forget to turn it off until much later. A simple, inexpensive timer switch will ensure the excess humidity is removed without unnecessarily running up your electric bill.

Top-loading washing machines emit a lot of moisture into the air, but front-loading machines do not, so if you plan to replace your washer, consider a front-loader. As noted in chapter 0, front-loading washers will also save energy and use a lot less water and detergent.

Building materials: things we bring in from outside

When renovating or remodeling a home, we have to accept the fact that we can't change everything. If we want a new kitchen and family room, we're not going to tear down the whole house, no matter what. But we might consider selectively replacing a few problematic materials from parts of the house that will remain essentially unchanged. For the most part, those won't be structural elements, so we'll deal with that in the next section. But we do have control of anything we add to the house.

Remodeling with nontoxic materials Here's the good news. With all the concerns about indoor air quality and toxic off-gassing, we are fortunate that it is now possible to find excellent

▲◄ Simple architectural details on this remodeled house in Massachusetts are effective means for preventing water intrusion. They include simple roof overhangs, a modest canopy over the rear entry, and properly installed flashing above each window.

▲► Rain gutters with downspouts that direct runoff well away from the foundation help ensure a dry basement, reducing the likelihood of problems with mold and mildew.

Carpets and rugs made from natural materials, like this 100% wool rug, are free from a variety of potentially harmful chemicals found in many synthetic carpets. The sealed-combustion gas fireplace provides warmth without degrading indoor air quality.

substitutes for just about anything that might contain harmful substances. There are more natural and nontoxic products and materials on the market than ever before. And they're getting easier to find all the time.

For purposes of simplification, we can group all the materials that go into remodeling a home into three broad categories: solids, fluids, and portables. Solids are the structural and fixed elements: lumber, plywood, insulation, cabinets, and anything else that becomes a permanent part of the structure. Fluids—or more precisely, things that start out in fluid form—include paint, wood finishes, caulks, and adhesives. These first two categories include all the stuff the house is actually built out of.

The third category, portables, includes carpeting, furniture, fabrics, wall coverings, and all the other decorative items that add to your home's beauty, comfort, and character. Like construction materials, these things can have a significant impact on your indoor air quality, too. But in this chapter, we'll focus on the first two categories; we'll look at portables in the next.

Yet another category of items that can affect your indoor air quality is cleaning products. These are used in all homes, of course, and don't have direct relevance to remodeling. But they do affect the air you breathe inside your home—remodeled or not (see the sidebar on p. 199 for some general recommendations). For now, let's stick with those things that are specific to remodeling.

Solids (structural materials) Until about 75 years ago, houses were built almost entirely from all-natural materials: wood, brick, stone, concrete, and so on. Wood came in the form of sawn lumber—trees that had passed through a sawmill with nothing added. Glue was made from animal or vegetable material. That remained largely unchanged until World War II, when technological advances, many of them first developed for military use, began finding their way into the private sector.

Plywood was used extensively in the construction of military barracks because it greatly sped up construction. By war's end, plywood quickly became one of the most common materials used in residential construction. Advances in chemistry soon made plywood stronger, more durable, and more water resistant. The miracle ingredient was formaldehyde. But the benefits of formaldehyde-based adhesives and resins came at a cost.

Today, formaldehyde is found not only in plywood but also in particleboard, OSB, engineered lumber like wood I-beams and LVLs, wood-veneered paneling, and laminated flooring. Many kitchen cabinets are made from particleboard boxes with doors and drawer fronts made from MDF. Particleboard has the second highest concentration of urea-formaldehyde of any engineered wood product. MDF has the highest.

Even some bamboo flooring, widely viewed as a signature green building material, may contain formaldehyde. The better brands of bamboo flooring are quite safe and do not contain added formaldehyde, but some of the lower-cost bamboo products may. Name-brand bamboo products usually have websites that include this information. If you have any doubts, ask to see the material safety data sheet (MSDS) before buying. As a general rule, it's best to avoid materials that do not have material safety data sheets.

Note the phrase, "added formaldehyde." All wood contains a certain amount of naturally occurring formaldehyde but in very low concentrations. It's the addition of formaldehyde-based binders, resins, and adhesives that poses health risks. Exposure to high levels of formaldehyde can cause asthma attacks and other respiratory symptoms, as well as headaches and nausea. It has also been shown to cause cancer in animals and may increase the risk of cancer in humans. There is no known safe level of formaldehyde, so it is best to avoid it as much as possible.

Materials made with phenol-formaldehyde off-gas at much lower levels than urea-formaldehyde. Construction-grade materials such as OSB sheathing made with phenol-formaldehyde are not

Painting and floor finishing are among the last steps in any remodeling project. Choosing low-VOC or (better still) zero-VOC products will help ensure a healthy living environment for your family.

generally considered to pose a health risk—especially as any off-gassing that does occur happens on the outside of the house rather than the inside.

Paints Although most building materials used prior to the middle of the last century were natural products containing few if any harmful chemicals, there was one notable exception: lead paint. Lead paint has been in continuous use since it was invented by the Dutch in the 17th century. Its toxic properties were well known by early in the 20th century, but lead paint was not banned in the United States until 1978.

Even after it was banned, existing stocks of lead paint still lingered on hardware store shelves. So to be safe, you should assume that any home built prior to 1980 might contain lead paint. Lead is only harmful if ingested or inhaled, so covering it over with a fresh coat of lead-free paint, sometimes referred to as encapsulation, is often the most practical and safest solution. However, if you have an older house where the old layers of paint are peeling or flaking off, this must be handled with care. Lead paint mitigation is beyond the scope of this book, but you can find more information at www.epa.gov/lead.

Today, the problem with paint comes not from lead but from VOCs. Paint containing VOCs can continue to off-gas for years, so you should avoid it as much as possible. There are a number of excellent brands of low-VOC and zero-VOC paint on the market now. Several of the best are from boutique companies like YOLO Colorhouse®, AFM Safecoat®, and Mythic. Most of the major paint companies now offer low- and zero-VOC products as well.

Another advantage of low-VOC paints is that there is little to no odor. This can be a big plus if you are living in the house while it is being painted.

Clear finishes A large percentage of remodeling jobs entail finishing hardwood floors. The most common floor finish used to be oil-based polyurethane. If you have ever been in a house soon after a coat of polyurethane went down, you probably remember the strong odor, which could take weeks to dissipate entirely. When you smell freshly finished floors, what you're smelling are volatile organic compounds. But as with paint, even after the odor is gone, VOCs continue to evaporate into the air for years.

Low-VOC floor finishes are now widely available, but the amount of VOCs vary. Floor finishes can be labeled "low-VOC" if they contain less than 350 g/L (grams per liter), but some have as little as 50 g/L. Zero-VOC finishes can also be found (see the sidebar on p. 195).

▼◄ **Zero-VOC paint from YOLO Colorhouse, in crisp, cheerful colors, brightens up this inexpensive kitchen remodel.**

▼▶ **The owner of this remodeled home selected breathable, PVC-free wallpapers printed with water-based inks and installed with a starch-based, nontoxic adhesive. Vinyl wall coverings off-gas VOCs and can trap humidity, creating a risk of mold growth.**

The pungent smell of freshly coated hardwood floors tells you that you are inhaling high concentrations of VOCs as they evaporate from the finish. If you use low-VOC or zero-VOC floor finishes instead, your floors will look just as good and you will eliminate a potential health risk for your family.

Natural oils, such as linseed and tung oil, are virtually free of VOCs, but they are sometimes thinned with solvents that do contain VOCs. If you want to be absolutely sure, read the label and ask for the MSDS (for most products, the MSDS can be found online).

Caulks and adhesives It is a rare remodeling project that doesn't entail the use of caulk or adhesives. Some of these contain high levels of VOCs, but, as with paints, stains, and floor finishes, you can now find low-VOC caulks and adhesives. You might not find them on the shelves of every hardware store yet, but many retailers are now carrying them. Here is where a little consumer activism goes a long way. If you can't find healthy building materials where you usually shop, tell them you'll find someplace that does.

A special note to do-it-yourselfers: You should be aware that off-gassing for any fluid material containing VOCs is dramatically higher during application.

Clean is green. A well-designed mudroom serves as a transition between outside and inside. Providing a convenient place for the family and even guests to remove their shoes upon entering can help keep pollutants from being tracked into the main living spaces.

green view

OSB, plywood, LVLs, and most other engineered wood products, including particleboard and MDF, are now available with no added formaldehyde, urea, or phenol. These are far preferable for any use inside the home. If your remodel doesn't include replacing wood products made with formaldehyde, you can reduce the risk of exposure by coating such materials with polyurethane (low-VOC polyurethane, of course), taking care to cover all exposed surfaces and edges.

Keeping it clean

Believe it or not, one of the simplest ways to keep pollutants out of the house is to take off your shoes. We track all sorts of things into our homes on the soles of our shoes—dust, germs, chemicals, etc. Providing a convenient place to remove them can keep your home cleaner and healthier. A mudroom or entry vestibule with a bench and a durable, easy-to-clean floor is ideal. But something as simple as a chair or stool by the door will work, too.

A well-maintained HVAC system with sealed ductwork can also keep your house cleaner. Correctly designed systems will provide balanced or even slightly positive air pressure inside the house. But leaky ducts—especially if they leak air into unconditioned spaces—tend to depressurize the home's interior relative to the outdoor air pressure. The result is that outdoor pollutants are drawn in through any open door or window. Sealing leaky air ducts not only saves you money by increasing energy efficiency but also can help keep your house cleaner.

VENTILATION

Another way we can help ensure good indoor air quality is by paying attention to the way our homes breathe. As we discussed in chapter 4, tightly sealed homes require controlled ventilation. While an old, drafty home might go through eight air changes per hour, the recommended amount of ventilation to maintain good air quality is eight changes in 24 hours.

Even in homes with whole-house ventilation systems, point-of-use ventilation in kitchens and bathrooms is still important. In the kitchen, you want to have a vent hood above the stove to remove fumes and excess humidity from cooking. The least expensive models often contain charcoal filters and merely recirculate the same air over and over. These won't do the trick. To do the job right, your vent hood should be vented directly to the outdoors.

HOW LOW IS LOW?

What, exactly, does "low-VOC" mean? The answer is somewhat complex because it means different things for different materials. Interior paint can carry the Green Seal label if it has a VOC content less than 50 g/L for flat wall paint or 150 g/L for nonflat finishes. For purposes of comparison, the maximum allowable VOC levels for paint sold in the United States is currently 250 g/L for flat finishes and 380 g/L for higher-luster finishes.

Can we get to absolute zero? Not all materials function ideally with zero VOCs. Depending on the application, some materials that are considered "low-emitting" have higher VOC content than others. The chart below is a summary of maximum VOC content (expressed in grams per liter) to qualify as low-emitting under the LEED guidelines.

MAXIMUM VOC CONTENT FOR "LOW-VOC" PRODUCTS

MATERIAL	VOC LIMIT (G/L)
Carpet adhesive	50
Wood flooring adhesive	100
Ceramic tile adhesive	65
Structural wood adhesive	140
Countertop adhesive	250
Flat paint and primer	50
Nonflat paint	150
Clear wood finishes:	
Varnish	350
Lacquer	550
Floor coating	100
Stains	250

A range hood that is vented directly to the outside, as in this green kitchen remodel, improves indoor air quality by removing fumes and excess humidity from cooking.

The garage is another potential source of harmful gases. If your garage is connected to living space, you should consider adding a small exhaust fan. The fan should be wired to turn on when the garage door opens and run for 10 to 15 minutes.

Combustion safety

Any combustion device or appliance needs to be properly vented to prevent dangerous fumes from mixing with our breathable air supply. Improperly vented fireplaces, woodstoves, furnaces, and water heaters can introduce noxious gases like carbon monoxide and nitrogen dioxide into the home, as well as particulate matter that can irritate the lungs.

Fireplaces and woodstoves need properly sized flues to maintain adequate draft. If at all possible, these should also have a dedicated air supply to prevent backdrafting. This is especially important in tightly sealed homes.

Your furnace should be professionally checked to make sure the flue pipe is properly installed and sealed and that the heat exchanger is not cracked. If you plan to replace your furnace or water heater, look for a sealed-combustion unit that doesn't allow combustion gases to mix with the indoor air supply.

AIR FILTERS AND CLEANERS

Residential air filters come in a variety of types and sizes. Some, like pleated furnace filters, are inexpensive, while whole-house air-cleaning systems cost considerably more. Both types are designed for removing particulates from the air as opposed to gaseous pollutants such as formaldehyde and other VOCs. The effectiveness of air filters is measured by minimum efficiency reporting value (MERV) ratings. The higher the number, the better the filter.

Some residential air filters have MERV ratings as high as 16, but filters rated above MERV 12 generally require specialized HVAC systems designed to handle the high air resistance such filters generate. For most homes, filters in the range of MERV 8 to 12 will do an excellent job at removing most airborne particulates as small as 0.3 microns, the size of mold spores.

If someone in your family suffers from asthma or allergies, you'll want an air filter at the high end of that range, say, MERV 11, which is at least 85% efficient at removing airborne particles as small as 3 microns. (Most of the remaining 15% of particles will be captured on subsequent passes through the filter.) For even more pristine air, you might want to consider an electrostatic air cleaner. Using an electrical field to trap tiny particles, the best electrostatic air cleaners can eliminate up to 99% of pollen and mold spores, 98% of bacteria-sized particles, and up to 80% of virus-sized particles.

HEPA filters—originally invented as part of the Manhattan Project to remove radioactive particles from the air—remove 99.97% of particles 0.3 microns in size, which is equal to a MERV rating of 17 to 20. True HEPA filters are used primarily in hospitals and in manufacturing processes that require extremely pure air. Some residential products are advertised as HEPA-type or HEPA-like filters; these are not really HEPA filters at all. When shopping for an air filter, ignore such hype and look for the MERV ratings.

Nature's air filters

In the late 1980s while investigating methods of purifying the air aboard space stations, NASA discovered that common houseplants can be quite useful in this regard. The NASA study showed that many houseplants are efficient at removing harmful chemicals such as benzine, trichloroethylene, and formaldehyde from the air.

Most species commonly used as houseplants are native to the understory of tropical forests where light levels are low. For that reason, they evolved to be very efficient at photosynthesis, which enables them to absorb larger quantities of CO_2 and emit more oxygen. This same trait enables them to absorb and process other gasses as well.

The study found that the best plants for removing chemical pollutants include English ivy, gerbera daisies, pot mums, peace lily, bamboo palm, mother-in-law's tongue, dracaena marginata, golden pathos, and green spider plants. NASA recommends using 15 to 18 plants to purify the air in a house of around 2,000 sq. ft.

MERV *WHO?*

Minimum efficiency reporting value (MERV) ratings measure how efficient an air filter is at removing airborne particles. The higher the number, the better the filter. The fiberglass filters that come with most furnaces have low MERV ratings—4 or less—which means they can trap only the largest airborne particles. These might protect the furnace but don't do much for indoor air quality. You can get a slight improvement by replacing these with 1-in. pleated filters, which have a MERV rating of 6. But for a significant improvement in indoor air quality, you'll want a 5-in. pleated filter rated at MERV 8 or higher.

PLEATED FILTER

Pleated air filters provide a lot of surface area for the air to pass through the filtration material. The deeper the pleats, the greater the surface area.

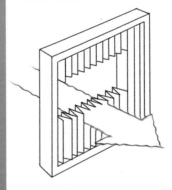

GREEN VACUUMING

If your remodeling budget will allow, a central vacuum system, vented to the outdoors, prevents dust and other contaminants from being merely redistributed, as happens with many portable vacuum cleaners. Or choose a portable vacuum cleaner with a high-efficiency particulate air (HEPA) filter. HEPA filters remove 99.9% of particles as small as 0.3 microns. Many vacuums are advertised as having "HEPA-type" filters. They may look the same but only capture 80% to 90% of particles that size. A true HEPA filter will have a label certifying its performance and bearing a serial number.

Asthma and allergy sufferers will benefit greatly from a cleaner house. Removing dust, pollen, pet dander, dust mites, and other irritants either with an externally vented central vacuum system or a portable vacuum cleaner with a HEPA filter can offer a noticeable reduction in symptoms.

When people ask me about making their homes greener, most of the time what they mean is more energy efficient and, perhaps, less polluting. But of the three fundamentals of green remodeling, creating a healthy living environment inside that energy-efficient, environmentally friendly home may have the most profound and far-reaching impact on the individual lives of the homeowners and their families.

Creating a healthy home doesn't end the day the remodeling project is finished, however. What we bring into the completed house matters, too. It would be a shame to follow all the recommendations for green remodeling with diligence and then fill the house with furniture and other objects that emit all of the same pollutants we worked so hard to banish in the first place. That is the topic I'll cover in the final chapter.

Common houseplants can be highly effective at purifying air. NASA studied the effectiveness of dozens of species for use aboard space stations, but they work just as well down here on earth.

GREEN CLEANING PRODUCTS

A substantial proportion of indoor air pollution stems not from building materials but from things we bring into our homes. And some of the most toxic substances we bring in are, paradoxically, the very products we use to keep the place clean. Here is a partial list of cleaners to avoid and a few safer alternatives.

ANTIBACTERIAL HOUSEHOLD CLEANERS, DISHWASHING LIQUID, AND HAND SOAPS

- Using these products can create resistant strains of bacteria.
- They don't make us any healthier. According to a study by Columbia University, there was no difference in the rate of illness between households that used antibacterial soaps and detergents and those that didn't.
- They create ecological hazards; after going down the drain, they persist in the environment, where they can accumulate in insects, birds, and fish.

Safer alternatives:
- Soap and water and a little elbow grease are highly effective at removing germs.
- Hydrogen peroxide works just fine as a disinfectant, and it doesn't cause any environmental damage because it breaks down safely into water and oxygen.
- Tea tree oil is a safe, natural biocide that is effective even when highly diluted.

CHLORINE BLEACH

- It is harmful if the vapors are inhaled.
- It can combine with organic matter to form a variety of toxins, some of which are known carcinogens.
- Wastewater containing chlorine bleach can cause environmental problems.

Safer alternatives:
- Chlorine-free bleach, also called oxygen bleach, contains hydrogen peroxide.
- Sunshine: Hanging clothes to dry in the sun leaves clothing looking brighter and smelling nicer.

LAUNDRY DETERGENTS CONTAINING FRAGRANCES, ALKYPHENOLS, OR PHOSPHATES

- Fragrances can trigger allergies or asthma.
- Alkyphenols are endocrine disrupters that are considered persistent organic pollutants.
- Phosphates end up in waterways where they cause algae blooms that deplete oxygen from the water, killing fish and other wildlife.

Safer alternatives:
- Use natural detergents containing no phosphates, chlorine, or fabric brighteners.
- Use laundry aids such as borax or washing soda (but this can damage silk or wool).

SPONGES

- Sponges are ideal breeding grounds for bacteria. Studies have shown that the average kitchen sponge contains far more dangerous bacteria than toilets in the same house.
- Wiping your counters with a damp sponge just spreads the bacteria around.
- Cleaning sponges in the dishwasher is not effective. Most dishwashers don't get hot enough, and the sponge always stays moist, which bacteria just love.

Safer alternatives:
- Boiling is the best way to disinfect sponges. Four minutes in a bowl of water in the microwave will do the trick.
- Use a fresh, dry dish cloth each time you wash dishes, then throw it in the laundry hamper.

DISHWASHER DETERGENTS CONTAINING CHLORINE OR PHOSPHORUS, BOTH OF WHICH CAUSE SERIOUS HARM TO WATERWAYS

Safer alternative:
- Use environmentally friendly dishwasher detergents made with enzymes, borax, or sodium carbonate (washing soda).

ADDING A WARM CAP TO A DRAFTY BUNGALOW

BEFORE

▲▶ Large sheets of flat, prefinished HardiePanel with galvanized z-flashing clad the upper floor at a fraction of the cost of standard siding. The original stucco was retained for the first floor.

It was a cozy one-story cottage on a lovely tree-shaded street within easy walking distance of schools, shopping, and parks. But it was not nearly large enough for a growing family, and the house leaked heat like a sieve. The owners, Ottar and Anna, loved their south Minneapolis home and neighborhood but needed more space and they had to do it on a budget. Oh, yes. And they wanted it to be green.

Working closely with his clients, architect Bryan Anderson of SALA Architects in Minneapolis listened to the couple's wish list and came up with a strategy. The plan was to provide a high-performing shell finished in simple and affordable materials to enclose the most space at the lowest cost. They would build up over existing space rather than spreading out, making the existing foundation perform double duty.

ADDING UP

On the first floor, the home's original stucco exterior was preserved. Above it, the new second story is clad with prefinished 4x8 sheets of HardiePanel®, a durable, maintenance-free fiber-cement siding material, installed with galvanized steel z-flashing, creating a stylish street presence at one-sixth the cost of traditional siding.

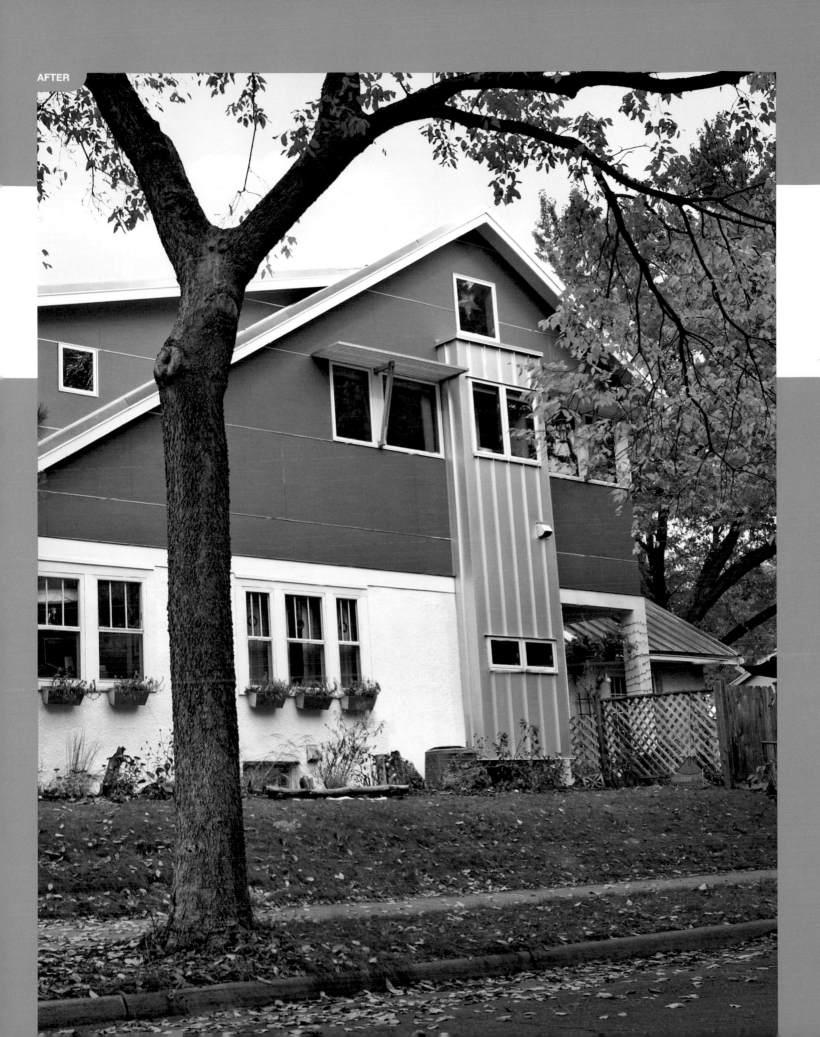

PROJECT AT A GLANCE

Originally built: 1920

Original size: 1,180 sq. ft.

Space after remodel: 1,900 sq. ft.

Architect: Bryan Anderson, SALA Architects

Location: Minneapolis, Minnesota

FIRST FLOOR (BEFORE)

FIRST FLOOR (AFTER)

The new second story added three bedrooms and two baths in 720 sq. ft., including circulation and storage space. The complete overhaul of the first floor reconfigured the interior living space and enclosed an unheated porch that became a playroom and home office. Gutting the interior walls made possible the addition of closed-cell sprayed foam insulation throughout, creating a tight thermal envelope that minimized air infiltration and dramatically reduced heat loss.

HEALTHY INDOOR AIR

With one toddler and a baby on the way, the owners were naturally concerned about creating a healthy indoor environment for their children. Low-emitting materials, including SkyBlend™ formaldehyde-free particleboard, zero-VOC paints and finishes, and low-VOC adhesives, were selected to avoid introducing harmful chemicals into the family's home. Formaldehyde-free MDF with a low-emitting clear finish was used as a decorative element to create a unique stairway that added architectural heft without costing a lot of money.

In tightly sealed homes, ventilation is essential for healthy indoor air quality. A heat-recovery ventilator (HRV) was installed to provide a continuous supply of fresh air to the interior while conserving the energy in the stale exhaust air. To further enhance air quality, easy-to-clean bare floors with small area rugs were selected instead of wall-to-wall carpet, which tends to trap a variety of indoor pollutants.

In the end, the clients' willingness to do much of the work themselves, including installation of the standing-seam galvanized roof and IKEA kitchen cabinets, was key to accomplishing their space and design goals without overspending. They managed to stick to their budget, nearly double their living space, and cut their heating bills by 40%.

Renovating this city home rather than moving enabled the owners to capitalize on the existing site in a dense, walkable neighborhood with a variety of community resources and easy access to public transportation. That was the most sustainable choice of all.

An open-plan kitchen, living room, and dining room makes the interior space bright and airy. Well-placed openings promote good cross ventilation, which saves money on air-conditioning costs.

▲◄ Making more out of less, formaldehyde-free MDF was used as a decorative material on walls and as cladding for the architectural stair and railing.

▲▶ A bookcase built into the stair landing makes the same space serve two purposes.

◄▲ In the kitchen, Energy Star appliances and lighting from compact fluorescent bulbs keep energy use down. The countertops are Richlite, a composite material made from recycled paper.

* Efficient space planning creates ample living space in a smaller package.

* A tight building envelope insulated with high-density sprayed foam has minimal air infiltration and heat loss.

* Durable exterior materials include prefinished, low-maintenance fiber-cement siding.

* A galvanized, standing-seam roof deflects excessive solar heat to minimize cooling needs.

* Rapidly renewable/recycled content materials used include:

  * Richlite composite countertops
  * Cork flooring
  * Linoleum flooring

* The open, airy interior provides ample daylight and good cross ventilation.

* Efficient lighting and appliances are used.

* Low-emitting materials include formaldehyde-free MDF and particleboard, as well as zero-VOC paints and finishes.

* Marvin Integrity® windows with low-E, argon-filled glazing were manufactured less than 500 miles from the building site.

* The home has a centralized hot-water distribution system and dual-flush toilets.

Custom-designed shading devices made of galvanized metal keep the sun from overheating the bedrooms in summer while admitting full sunlight in winter.

9 GREEN INSIDE AND OUT

In the previous chapters, I have focused on the permanent, fixed parts of the house—the bricks and sticks, HVAC system, things that use water and electricity, and pretty much everything that is nailed down, glued down, brushed on, screwed or bolted in place, or otherwise physically attached to the home's structure. But now that you've gone to the effort and expense of remodeling your house, making it more energy efficient, healthier to live in, and easier on the environment—in short, greener—is that all there is to think about?

Once the dust has settled, the paint is dry, and the workers have packed up their tools and gone home, it's time to begin actually living in your freshly remodeled home. But what about all the things you bring into the house— furniture, rugs, draperies, and the like? What are they made from and where do they come from? Do they have any effect on your indoor environmental quality or on the global environment we all share? And what happens when you go outside? Does green remodeling concern itself with landscaping?

For a client sensitive to the kind of contaminants that can get lodged in rugs or carpeting, the interior designer for this sunroom added visual interest by stenciling a pattern on the floor—with nontoxic paint and sealed with a zero-VOC clear finish.

As it turns out, everything matters. Just as we needed to consider how each part of the house affects all the other parts and how, together, they all have an impact on sustainability—or greenness, if you will—what you put in and around the house is also part of the larger picture. Let's start with the inside and then conclude by stepping outside and taking a walk around the house.

GREEN DECORATING

Your remodeling project is nearly finished. A few touch-ups with zero-VOC paint are all that remain to be done. You've already outlawed building materials containing formaldehyde and other VOCs, installed high-efficiency air filters, got humidity under control, and, in the kitchen, added a vent hood ducted to the outside to carry fumes away from the gas range.

High-performance insulation and a tightly sealed building envelope keep heat loss to a bare minimum. The shell is so energy efficient that only a very small heating plant is needed. And to do that job, you chose a sealed-combustion, high-efficiency furnace or boiler that doesn't allow the by-products of combustion to mix with indoor air, or perhaps you decided to eliminate combustion systems altogether and installed a geothermal heat pump. To boost efficiency further, you had the ducts sealed to eliminate air leakage, which has the added benefit of balancing air pressure inside the house so dust and pollen aren't sucked in through every open window and door. You've even provided a place to take off your shoes when entering the house to avoid tracking pollutants in from the street.

Then the van from the furniture store pulls up and delivers, along with your new furniture, drapes, and carpeting, a whopping dose of alphabet soup (see chapter 8). Sadly, a lot of home furnishings contain chemicals we would not choose to inhale if we had any say in the matter. Wood furniture made from particleboard—usually with a wood or laminate veneer—and MDF may contain significant amounts of formaldehyde. Vinyl upholstery and floor and wall coverings off-gas phthalates, which are known endocrine disrupters and can cause a variety of respiratory ailments. Upholstery fabrics, rugs, draperies, foam cushions, and mattresses often contain polybrominated diphenyl ethers (PBDEs), a class of brominated flame-retardants (BFRs) that are also found in the plastic outer shells of computers, TVs, and other home electronics. PBDEs can account for up to 15% of some plastics and 27% of upholstery fabrics by weight.

According to the nonprofit organization Environmental Working Group, PBDEs can disrupt the body's thyroid hormone balance "by depressing levels of the T3 and T4 hormones, which are important to normal metabolism. In adults, hypothyroidism can cause fatigue, depression, anxiety, unexplained weight gain, hair loss, and low libido." This is scary stuff, but knowledge is power. Armed with information about exactly what we don't want in our home furnishings, we can begin to look for safer alternatives. Knowing what questions to ask is half the battle.

Choosing healthy furnishings

When buying upholstered furniture, look for frames made from sustainably harvested hardwood assembled with water-based biodegradable glues and non-VOC finishes. For the upholstery, look for foam padding made with soy or natural latex foam rubber and fabrics made from natural fibers and nontoxic dyes.

Control dust mites and other allergens

If anyone in your home suffers from allergies or asthma, controlling dust, pet dander, and dust mites is essential. Wall-to-wall carpeting is highly effective at collecting those things and no amount of vacuuming will eliminate them. As you walk across a carpeted room, each step you take releases little clouds of those allergens into the air. Unlike wall-to-wall carpeting, hardwood, tile, and linoleum floors are a snap to keep clean and dust-free. In rooms where you want something softer underfoot, area rugs can offer color and comfort and can be easily removed for a thorough cleaning.

Draperies provide another place for dust to settle and hide. Instead, you might consider nonfabric alternatives. Wood blinds or plantation shutters can be easily wiped down to remove dust, and they can be adjusted to control daylight and privacy to suit your needs.

But does any of this mean we'll be consigned to strange-looking or uncomfortable furniture? Do we need to forgo beautiful things? Do we have to give up luxury? Not at all. There are now numerous sources for safe, healthy, and beautiful alternatives in all styles and price ranges. As Trudy Dujardin, an interior designer who specializes in sustainable interiors, likes to say, a healthy home is the ultimate luxury.

The living room couch in this Harlem brownstone has a frame of FSC-certified alder wood with water-based stains and glue, and cushions of natural latex and down, covered in fabric made from all-natural fibers. The end tables, by Scrapile, are made from discarded scraps of wood from New York's woodworking industry. The bamboo flooring is easy to keep free of dust and other allergens that can collect in carpeting. The natural clay plaster wall finish does not off-gas and never needs painting.

green view

Advocates of healthy eating will tell you that the foods that are best for you are the ones containing the fewest ingredients. The same advice can be applied to furniture and fabrics for the home. There are more than 8,000 chemicals commonly used in the textile industry. Many of them have known toxic properties, and most of them have never been tested for their effects on humans. Most synthetic fabrics contain dozens of ingredients, many of which are not even identified on the label. Wool has one ingredient. Organic cotton has one ingredient. But even with natural fibers, dyes add more ingredients to the finished product, so look for fabrics made with vegetable-based dyes.

GREEN IN BED

You spend a third of your life in bed. But what is your bed made of? Is the mattress made with foam or covered in material containing brominated flame-retardants? Is the frame or headboard upholstered in a material that off-gases formaldehyde? And what about your sheets and blankets? Surely your linens can't be harmful—or can they? A lot of the fabrics used for bedding, including mattresses, pillows, sheets, and blankets, are treated with pesticides, herbicides, flame-retardants, and stain-resistant solvents, not to mention the potentially worrisome substances in many synthetic fibers.

Here are some tips for making your bed a truly restorative, healthful place to spend 8 or so hours out of every 24.

- Look for mattresses made from natural latex, wool, and organic cotton. If you are not replacing your mattress but have concerns about what it is made from, you can cover it with a cotton barrier cloth encasing.

- Learn to love wrinkles. Permanent-pressed sheets and pillowcases are treated with formaldehyde, which has been associated with such symptoms as headaches, eye and respiratory irritation, gastrointestinal problems, and sleep disturbance, even at very low levels of exposure.

- Choosing natural fibers is always a good idea—wool is naturally fire resistant, so it is not treated with flame-retardants. But most sheep are regularly dipped with pesticides to control parasites, so look for organic wool or cotton bedding.

- If you are allergic to dust mites, use mattress and pillow covers made from cotton barrier cloth. Avoid the plastic covers made for this purpose—they,

themselves may outgas chemicals, replacing one problem with another.

- Choose pillows made from goose down or wool (unless you are allergic to these materials).

Many people believe that electromagnetic fields (EMFs) have harmful effects, especially with long periods of exposure. While this is somewhat controversial, avoiding EMFs certainly won't do you any harm and may be safer. If you are concerned about EMF exposure while you sleep, here are some steps you can take:

- Keep digital clocks, televisions, computers, and anything that uses a transformer—like cell-phone chargers—at least 6 ft. from the bed.

- The transformers in halogen lamps give off much stronger EMFs. Better to keep them far from the bed or out of the bedroom altogether.

- Do not use electric blankets. You can be subjected to electromagnetic fields even when they are turned off. For the same reason, avoid waterbeds—they also have electric heating elements.

The owners of this remodeled Harlem, New York, brownstone rest easy in the knowledge that even their bed is as green as possible. The frame is made from FSC-certified wood and assembled with nontoxic adhesives and finish. The headboard is upholstered with wool batting and natural fibers. Organic cotton sheets and bedspread cover a mattress made with natural latex foam and organic cotton.

Covering all the bases, the owner of this house on Nantucket Island re-modeled using multiple strategies for creating a healthy living environment. The kitchen range hood is vented to the outside to remove excess humidity and fumes from cooking. Mostly bare floors, with an area rug of natural sisal, make it easy to keep the space dust-free. Zero-VOC paint and wood finishes were used exclusively, and the furniture is made with nontoxic adhesives and upholstered with latex foam cushions and natural, organic fabrics.

SUSTAINABLE LANDSCAPING: ISN'T IT ALREADY GREEN OUTSIDE?

The project has finally come to an end. Following all of the advice in this book, your freshly remodeled house, along with everything in it, is as green as green can be. But does going green stop at the outside walls? Open the door and step outside, into the front yard. What could be greener than this? The sun is shining. Birds are singing in the trees. Flowers are blooming. And the lawn—our pride and joy—the lawn is perfection, not a weed to be seen. Ah, nature!

Of course, we can't give nature all the credit. It took hard work to get it looking this way—hours of mowing and weeding and trimming; spreading fertilizer and weed killer; and more fertil-izer. And water—lots and lots of water. How did nature manage without us all these years?

Grass isn't always greener

The American lawn, that lush carpet of green that is the icon of suburbia, did not always exist. Odd as the thought may seem to our modern worldview, this uniform swath of emerald is a complete fabrication, something not found in nature. Somehow, however, we have come to accept the inevitability of lawn care. We love our lawns. We must—why else would we devote such vast amounts of time, effort, and expense to cultivating an estimated 20 million acres of this industrial monoculture? Without questioning why, we enthusiastically water, weed, fertilize, and mow in pursuit of a more perfect lawn than our neighbors.

Yet lawns are also an environmental nightmare. The millions of tons of chemical fertilizers and weed killers that we apply have high environmental costs. They wash off our lawns and run into our wells, streams, and lakes, wreaking havoc with aquatic ecosystems and turning up in our food supply and drinking water.

Grass clippings that are bagged and hauled away clog our landfills, and the watering of lawns depletes critically scarce water supplies. In our zeal to eradicate the lowly dandelion, we blithely pour poison onto the soil and then watch our children and pets gamboling on that grassy patch of green we call the backyard, all the while feeling grateful to be raising our family in the safe, healthy, leafy suburbs. It doesn't even occur to us that there might be an alternative.

Sustainable alternatives

There are many ways to reduce the negative environmental impacts of our lawns and gardens. One of the easiest is to reduce the size of the lawn. Instead of automatically planting grass everywhere, consider planting the perimeter of the property as a wildflower meadow, which only needs to be cut once per year. Other areas can be planted with groundcovers like pachysandra or myrtle, which, once established, need virtually no care or watering. There are dozens of types of groundcovers available to meet different needs. Your local garden center is likely to have a selection that is suited to the local climate. Many more varieties are available online.

What about growing food instead of grass? You might consider turning part of your property into a vegetable garden. Growing some of your own food can be highly satisfying, and there's nothing like the taste of freshly picked produce.

Mowing your lawn is not only bad for the environment. As you push that power mower around your property, you are inhaling a not-so-healthy dose of hydrocarbons, carbon monoxide, and

green view

Power motors contribute to air pollution and global warming. American homeowners consume 800 million gallons of gas each year, just by mowing their lawns. According to the Environmental Protection Agency, one gas-powered lawn mower produces as much air pollution per hour as 11 cars; riding mowers pollute as much as 34 cars.

One power mower spews as much pollution into the air as 11 cars, and you inhale a lot of that pollution as you push the mower around your lawn.

particulate matter—none of which does your respiratory system any good. Reducing the size of your lawn means less water, fewer chemicals, and less maintenance. And as your lawn gets smaller, cutting the grass with a push-type reel mower becomes quite practical. Push mowers produce no pollution, and the soft whirring sound they make as they scissor the blades of grass is infinitely more pleasant to listen to on a Sunday afternoon than the roar of a power mower. Newer models operate with little effort. A good rule of thumb for a sustainable lawn is that the total turf area should be small enough that you can easily maintain it with a manual push mower.

Lawns are also very thirsty. From 2002 to 2007, municipal water rates have increased by an average of 27% in the United States, 32% in the United Kingdom, 45% in Australia, 50% in South Africa, and 58% in Canada. The amount of water our lawns and gardens consume is related not only to the size of our lawns but also to the type of plants we cultivate. As landscaping is extremely climate sensitive, choosing plant species that are native to your geographic location will cut down your water usage. These plants have adapted, through evolution, to thrive in local soils and on the amount of rainfall typical to the area.

Preserving wildlife habitat is another sustainable landscaping choice. The suburbs were shaped by zoning regulations that favor large building lots. This came about partly from a desire to preserve open space. Unfortunately, large-lot zoning had the opposite effect. Dividing up the landscape into quarter-acre or half-acre (or larger) lots effectively eliminates the natural habitat for thousands of species.

Much of the water from spray heads is lost to evaporation. For flower beds and vegetable gardens, drip irrigation makes a better choice. Applying water directly to the ground strengthens root systems and uses much less water.

By minimizing the hegemony of turf grass, we can restore some of that lost habitat while making our yards more beautiful, more interesting, and easier and cheaper to maintain. And choosing plants that provide food and shelter will attract a variety of colorful songbirds, adding interest and delight and keeping insect populations in check without the use of insecticides.

Harvesting rain

When we talk about saving water, what we really mean is conserving potable water—water that is pure enough for drinking. Considering the critical problem of water scarcity, we might reasonably question the wisdom of pouring such a valuable commodity on the ground or using it to flush toilets, which accounts for about a quarter of indoor water use.

green view

For parts of the garden that do require irrigation, there are a number of ways to conserve water. Watering lawns early in the morning reduces the evaporation that would occur in the heat of the day, when as much as half the water sprayed into the air never reaches the ground. For shrubs and flower beds, drip irrigation, which applies water directly to the roots, eliminates waste through runoff and evaporation and keeps plants well hydrated using much less water. For larger properties, consider a smart irrigation controller, which monitors weather data from satellites and automatically calculates watering requirements for different zones of the garden. If the controller knows rain is likely on Wednesday, it won't water the lawn on Tuesday.

The front yard of this net-zero energy remodel in California is planted almost entirely in drought-resistant, low-maintenance plants, with only a small plot of grass for decorative purposes.

PUTTING TREES TO WORK: LANDSCAPING FOR PASSIVE SOLAR BENEFITS

Creating a pleasant outdoor environment is one of the joys of good landscaping. But trees and shrubs can serve another purpose as well. They can boost your home's energy efficiency by helping you capture passive solar benefits. With a little attention to what you plant and where you plant it, your landscaping can keep your house cooler in summer and allow the sun to warm it in winter.

Deciduous trees (the kind that lose their leaves in winter), especially when planted on the east and west sides, will help keep the sun from overheating your house during the hottest months of the year; when the weather turns colder, they conveniently drop their leaves and allow the sun's warming rays through. On the north side of the house, a stand of evergreen trees will block cold winter winds that rob your house of heat.

Air-conditioning units sitting in the hot sun are less efficient at dissipating heat. Shading AC equipment with trees or shrubs can boost its efficiency by up to 10%. Unshaded paving absorbs heat from the sun and reradiates it back into the air after the sun goes down, making still more work for your air conditioner. In denser urban areas, this phenomenon, known as the heat island effect, can raise the temperature of whole neighborhoods, and even whole cities, by several degrees. (It has been estimated that the heat island effect costs the city of Los Angeles $100 million per year in added cooling costs.) Using landscaping to shade hard surfaces, such as driveways, walks, and patios, can increase indoor comfort and save you money by reducing air-conditioning loads.

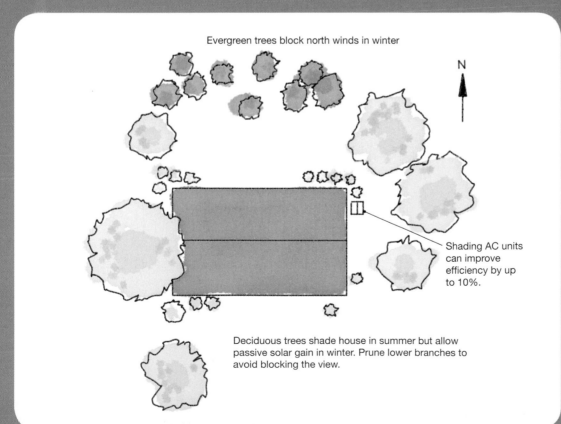

Evergreen trees block north winds in winter

N

Shading AC units can improve efficiency by up to 10%.

Deciduous trees shade house in summer but allow passive solar gain in winter. Prune lower branches to avoid blocking the view.

In any climate, selecting native species—plants that have naturally adapted to the soil conditions and the amount of local rainfall—can provide a beautiful, interesting, and sustainable respite from the ubiquitous American lawn. The front yard of this green remodel in Florida gets by quite well without regular watering. During especially dry spells, roof runoff captured in rain barrels is enough to keep plantings green and healthy.

Depending on where you live, outdoor water use can account for 50% to 80% of your total water consumption in the summer, which adds a considerable amount to your water and sewer bill. Yet free water falls from the sky on a regular basis. We might not always know when it is going to rain, but we do have a pretty accurate idea of how much rain falls annually in any given area. The problem is that it doesn't always rain when the lawn needs it, and when it does rain, much of the water goes to waste.

Rainwater harvesting captures excess runoff when it does rain and stores it for later use. It can be done quite simply and inexpensively using rain barrels placed beneath downspouts.

A hose attached to a spigot on the rain barrel can then be used for watering your garden. There are commercial rainwater-harvesting products available at every scale, from simple rain barrels to systems designed to capture and store thousands of gallons, often in underground tanks, which can be used for more substantial irrigation needs and even for flushing toilets.

Rain gardens

Sometimes the problem is too much water. Storm-water runoff can create problems with erosion and also places a strain on municipal storm drains and wastewater treatment plants. In many areas, when you enlarge your house you may be required to install drywells or infiltrators—underground structures that collect runoff and allow it to gradually seep into the soil. But for the same cost you might be able to solve the runoff problem and create a beautiful landscape feature at the same time.

Rain gardens are designed to absorb storm-water runoff like a giant sponge and slow it down so that it can percolate into the soil. Native plants that can survive dry periods as well as an inundation after a storm, with deep roots to soak up rainwater, are ideal choices. Rain gardens also provide valuable wildlife habitat, attracting birds, butterflies, and many other attractive species.

Sustainable landscaping reminds us that greener living doesn't all happen within the walls of our homes. Extending the concept of sustainability out into the natural world, or at least to the edge of the backyard, reminds us that we are all stewards of the earth. The choices we make every day have a collective impact on the health of this small blue marble we call home, and we can all take part in handing it over, in good condition, to the next generation.

▲◄ **For a remodeled house in Massachusetts, the landscape designer created a rain garden to absorb runoff from the patio and roof drains, which are tied into a 4-in. perforated pipe beneath a bed of beach rocks between the retaining wall and patio.**

▲▶ **Plant choices include *Eupatorium purpureum* (Joe Pye Weed), *Lobelia cardinalis* (Cardinal Flower), and *Aster novae-angliae* (New England Aster), which help cleanse the water of harmful pollutants before it seeps back into the groundwater table.**

GREEN REMODEL

A HARLEM BROWNSTONE GOES GREEN ON THE INSIDE

BEFORE

Starting from scratch: The house was little more than a shell when the owners found it. It took a leap of faith to imagine transforming it into a modern green home.

When Alicia and David, both actors with bicoastal careers, planned their move from Los Angeles to New York, they were looking for a nice two-bedroom apartment, either on Manhattan's Upper West Side or in Chelsea. But after looking at 120 apartments and not finding anything they liked at a price that made sense, a friend suggested looking farther north.

The 100-year-old brownstone they found in Harlem looked promising, but it needed a total gut renovation. There were holes in the roof and the interior was wet, moldy, and full of trash. "We hadn't planned on doing a lot of work," David said, "but when we found this house we could see what a great investment it would be."

Alicia insisted that if they were going to take on this much construction it had to be as green as possible. And David didn't need much convincing. With the help of designer Hannah Purdy and GreenStreet Construction, the couple began evaluating every aspect of the project in terms of sustainability. For every product or material that would be used in their house, the couple would always ask, "Is there a green alternative?"

COOL, GREEN, AND AFFORDABLE

"We learned a lot from them," Alicia said, "but I think they learned almost as much from us. Actors often have free time during the day, so we spent endless hours doing research on systems and materials, and figuring out where to find cool, different, green stuff that's also affordable."

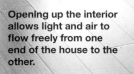

Opening up the interior allows light and air to flow freely from one end of the house to the other.

The mostly unchanged exterior belies the thoroughness of the total gut remodel that incorporated sustainability at every opportunity, turning this 100-year-old Harlem brownstone a deep shade of green.

For a built-in bookcase in the study, for example, Alicia placed an ad on Craigslist asking for eco designers who could create something unique for a totally green house. Within five minutes, she had a reply from four students at Pratt Institute, one of New York's premier design schools, who had just formed a business to make modern furniture out of reclaimed wood. The old water-tower wood they used has a rich, warm patina that was brought to life with all-natural nontoxic sealers. She was so pleased with the results that she had them make a bench for the entry vestibule, too.

TIGHTENING UP THE ENVELOPE

But woodworking, of course, came later. The first step in greening this house was to tighten up the building envelope to minimize heating and cooling loads. The windows were replaced with double-pane, argon-filled, low-e units, all of which had to be custom made because of the non-standard sizes. To reduce air leakage, expanding foam was used to seal around each window and exterior door and anywhere else where air infiltration might occur.

In row houses, adjacent homes provide a considerable amount of free insulation. As this was an end unit (which provides a big advantage in terms of daylight), insulation had to be added on the side where none existed before. But the owners were reluctant to cover up the handsome exposed brick walls in the living and dining areas. After considering several schemes, a solution was arrived at: Most of the wall would be framed out to provide a deep cavity for

A diaphanous window treatment affords privacy from the street but admits plenty of daylight to brighten the interior. The walls are finished in a subtly textured natural clay plaster that is free of chemicals and never needs painting. The flooring and the molded chair in the foreground are bamboo.

Daylight filters down from a skylight at the top of the stair. The light-colored wall to the left reflects sunlight deeper into the home's interior. Near the skylight, a whole-house fan (not shown) draws heat out of the house, reducing the need for air-conditioning.

insulation, while leaving four strategically located vertical strips of exposed brick. This dramatically increased the overall R-value of the wall without completely sacrificing the beauty of the brick wall's time-worn patina.

To further minimize heat loss, roof insulation was doubled. And to cut down on unwanted solar gain in summer, the old tar-coated flat roof was replaced with a white membrane that reflects the sun's heat away from the house. The white roof membrane has the added advantage of reducing an urban problem known as the heat island effect.

In warm weather, passive stack ventilation provided by a rooftop mushroom vent located above the stair tower helps keep the house cool. On warmer days, a mechanical whole-house fan draws hot air out of the house. Ceiling fans in the living room and bedrooms also help keep the interior quite comfortable using only natural ventilation. As a result, air-conditioning is needed only on summer's hottest days.

WARM UNDERFOOT

Heating and hot water are provided by a 95% efficient gas-fired Polaris® water heater. The heat is delivered to each room via radiant tubing under the floors. Zone controls make it possible to shut off rooms that are not being used.

The initial plan was to use Warmboard®, a plywood subfloor with heavy-gauge aluminum bonded to the top, with recessed grooves to accept PEX hot water tubing, but it didn't fit the

▲◄ The cheerful graffiti continues above the second floor where a wall of translucent sliding panels allows daylight from an exercise room and a guest room to illuminate the upstairs hall.

▲► The stair and railing are made from recycled steel. The owners leave out boxes of colored chalk for guests to write messages on the black painted metal. The stair treads are Eco-Terr®, terrazzo slabs made from recycled marble chips.

▲ In the third-floor master bedroom suite, a bar cabinet is
topped with a countertop of
recycled glass.

▶ A sealed-combustion gas fireplace quickly warms the master
bedroom while waiting for the
radiant floors to heat up.

budget. Looking for a more economical alternative, David found a company in Vermont that
could supply the materials for a similar application that he would be able to install himself. This
consisted of the same PEX tubing but affixed to the underside of the subfloor and secured with
molded aluminum sheets to evenly conduct the heat. After hand-stapling some 3,000 sheets of
aluminum and wearing out eight staple guns in the process, David finished the job, and the system works beautifully.

Asked if he would change anything if he had to do it over again, David confessed that he
probably would pay someone else to do the stapling or just go with the Warmboard, which he
thinks would be competitive if the cost of labor were factored in.

✳ Insulation was improved by sealing air leaks, and high-performance windows were installed.

✳ Highly-efficient space heating, aided by passive ventilation, reduces the need for air-conditioning.

✳ Efficient lighting and appliances include:

- CFLs in recessed lights
- Cove lighting with 6-ft. fluorescent tubes
- Appliances meet European energy standards, which are stricter than Energy Star.

✳ Reclaimed and rapidly renewable materials include:

- Stair railing made from reclaimed steel
- Bamboo flooring

✳ Daylighting strategies were employed:

- Skylight at top of stairs
- Translucent sliding wall panels by Raydoor® allow sunlight from bedroom windows to illuminate the hallway.

✳ Low-emitting materials include:

- Zero-VOC paint and floor finish
- American Clay Plaster walls with integral color that don't need painting

✳ Green furnishings include:

- Molded bamboo chair by Modern Bamboo™
- Living room couch by Viesso® has a frame of FSC-certified alder wood with water-based stains and glue and cushions of natural latex and down that are covered in fabric made from all-natural fibers.
- End tables by Scrapile, made from discarded scraps of wood from New York's woodworking industry

A bar cabinet in the dining room is made from reclaimed Peroba wood from dismantled houses in Brazil.

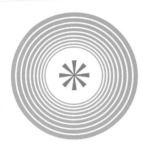

AFTERWORD

After paging through this book, you might still be left with a few questions. That was a lot of information, you might be thinking—how am I supposed to remember it all when I meet with my contractor? Do I really need to do all of those things to make my home green? And how green is green enough? I would answer as follows.

1. *How am I going to remember all that?* You do not need to remember all, or even any, of the specifics. What I hope you come away with is a general understanding of the kinds of issues that green remodeling deals with and enough familiarity with those issues to enable you to ask informed questions.

2. *Do I need to do everything?* No. You couldn't even if you wanted to. Every remodeling project is unique. As you think about your own home, some things will jump out at you as practical solutions that you definitely want to implement. It should also be fairly obvious which things are not appropriate in your situation. That leaves a third category—things that could be done, things that might be nice to do, but you are not sure exactly how far you want to go with this. For all of the things you are not sure about, see the next answer.

3. *How green is green enough?* First of all, keep in mind that there is no absolute standard. There are different shades of green; it's all a matter of degree. It takes a pretty serious commitment to make your home absolutely as deep green as is humanly possible. But green remodeling is not an all-or-nothing proposition. There are certainly some lighter shades of green that are both within your reach and genuinely more sustainable than most other homes. How, then, do we know where to draw the line between light green (though still legitimately green) and greenwashing?

To answer that, keep in mind the three fundamentals of green remodeling: energy efficiency, resource conservation, and healthy living environments. To repeat what I wrote in chapter 2, the bottom line is this: To call a remodel green, it needs to address each of the three fundamentals in some way. If it's not energy efficient, it's not green. If it doesn't conserve materials or water, or reduce the strain your home places on the environment, it's not green. And if it's not healthy to live in, it's not green.

IT'S NOT ROCKET SCIENCE

I have also tried to demonstrate that most of what constitutes green building is not mysterious, difficult, obscure, hard to find, or demanding of skill sets not available in today's workforce. A great deal of it is simply a matter of common sense, time-tested methods, and proper construction details. Yes, some of that seems to have been in short supply in recent decades; a lot of houses I've seen have convinced me that common sense isn't quite as common as it once was. But a resurgence of demand, from better informed consumers, for good old-fashioned quality, for doing things the right way, would go a long way toward making homes greener.

You don't need to be a scientist to understand that a drafty house is less comfortable and more expensive to heat. Find the gaps that let the breeze blow through your house, seal them up, and you've gone a long way toward improved energy efficiency.

You know that if you go outside on a frigid winter day barefoot or without a hat, you'll lose body heat pretty fast. So it isn't much of a jump to realize that beefing up your insulation—especially in the basement and attic—will help your home retain heat, too.

You've watched enough cartoons to know that the bottle labeled "poison" hiding behind the cat's back is likely to be bad news for the canary. So why not pay a little more attention to the list of chemicals found in the materials you use to remodel your home?

FINAL THOUGHTS

Throughout this book I have offered some general principles for green remodeling, along with more specific information about methods and materials that can be used to accomplish those principles. I have also attempted to provide some context for the reasons to consider these options, with the full knowledge that not every reason will be equally meaningful to every reader. An issue that is compelling to one group of homeowners may in other cases fall on deaf ears. But I have tried to provide enough examples of problems and solutions that every reader will find something to connect with and, I hope, find useful in their own home.

Much as I might wish it, I know that not every homeowner is equally concerned about environmental problems such as global warming. But it's very likely that, even among those who may be less alarmed about climate change, many will be particularly concerned with, for example, the potential effects of indoor air quality on their family's health. Others may not be as concerned with the effects of indoor air pollution, but may be passionate about social, political, environmental, or economic issues, such as global shortages of clean water, the loss of biodiversity in tropical rain forests, the effects of deforestation on indigenous peoples, or the geopolitical dangers that stem from our dependence on other countries, many of them hostile, for so much of the energy we consume every day. Building green addresses all these issues. There is truly something for everyone.

I have also tried to make the case that, even for those who don't buy any of the other arguments, making your home greener still makes sense because it will save you money. Everybody likes to save money.

What I haven't been able to come up with are any compelling arguments *against* building or remodeling green. Because, when it comes right down to it, building green is just another way of saying building better. I've never had a client ask me, "Isn't there a worse way to do this?" No one has ever asked me to be sure to incorporate some toxic materials so they can justify taking more sick days off of work. And no clients have ever asked me to try to make their utility bills higher.

So here is my bottom line—as a builder, as a homeowner, as a parent, and as a citizen of planet Earth. Once you know how to build or remodel a home in ways that make it more comfortable, less harmful to the environment, and less costly to operate and maintain, and that reduce its occupants' exposure to harmful substances, thereby making it more valuable on the real estate market—why on earth wouldn't you do that?

I had two aims in writing this book. One was to arm you with practical information that you can use to make your home greener—whether that means a comprehensive whole-house retrofit or just doing a few simple things to boost energy efficiency. The other was to inspire. Green remodeling entails doing things differently than business as usual. It requires a change in thinking. So in addition to explaining the nuts and bolts of the subject I thought it was important to provide some background on the kinds of issues that have already made greener living a compelling choice for so many people. If you did not count yourself among them before you picked up this book, I sincerely hope that you do now. If you have been sitting on the fence and I haven't quite managed to push you entirely over to the side where all things, not just the grass, are greener, I hope I have at least nudged you, however slightly, in that general direction.

APPENDIX

CONDUCTING AN ENERGY AUDIT

If your home is like most of the houses in this country, it is wasting a lot of energy. Heat is escaping through numerous gaps, small and large. You can locate many of these energy bandits yourself with a do-it-yourself energy audit. But there are also many problems that can only be detected through a professional energy audit. Let's first discuss what you can do on your own.

REDUCE AIR INFILTRATION

Here's where to look for the most common air leaks that are robbing you of expensively heated air:

* Weatherstripping around doors

* Windows that don't seal tightly and gaps around window frames

* Baseboards, switch plates, and electrical outlets (especially on exterior walls, but cold air from the basement can also be drawn in through interior walls)

* Wall-mounted or window-mounted air conditioners

* Attic hatches

* Ceiling penetrations such as recessed light fixtures

* The rim joist, which is the band of framing in the basement or crawl space that sits directly on top of the foundation

The best time to find which of these places are leaking air is when it's colder outside than it is indoors. Making sure all doors, windows, and fireplace flues are closed, turn on all the bathroom exhaust fans. If you have a range hood in the kitchen that vents to the outdoors, turn that on, too. This will depressurize the home slightly, drawing outside air in through all the small gaps you need to seal. You will be able to find where cold air is coming in by moving a stick of incense around suspect areas and watching the smoke. Or you can feel most leaks with a damp hand.

A blower door test depressurizes the interior of the home in order to find sources of air infiltration.

Once you find where cold air is coming in you can add weatherstripping where appropriate, adjust sash locks to keep windows closed tightly, and plug leaks with caulk or expanding foam. You can stop drafts from switches and outlets with inexpensive gaskets sold in most hardware stores.

TIGHTEN UP ATTIC PENETRATIONS

Caulk around air-conditioning vents and electrical boxes, and add foam weatherstripping around the attic hatchway. Seal gaps around pipes and ducts with fire-rated caulk or expanding foam. Large gaps around chimneys need to be sealed with sheet metal, which may not be a job for most do-it-yourselfers.

If you have recessed lights, first determine whether the fixtures are designed for insulated ceilings. These have an airtight metal box, or can, and an override switch to prevent overheating. If you can find the model number, look for the letters "IC," which indicates the fixture is rated for insulation contact. If the fixture is not IC rated, or you are not sure, you can't place insulation on top of the fixture and must keep insulation 3 in. away from the sides. In that case, consider replacing the fixtures with new IC-rated ones, or eliminate them and use ceiling-mounted fixtures or track lights.

LOOK FOR MISSING INSULATION

Conduct a visual inspection of the insulation in your attic and basement. Add or replace missing insulation *after* sealing gaps. Don't count on fiberglass batts to stop air flow.

PROFESSIONAL ENERGY AUDITS

A professional energy audit will look for sources of air infiltration in all the places mentioned above, but with sophisticated equipment that can do a more thorough job. It will also locate sources of heat loss that can't be seen with the naked eye. When hiring an energy auditor make sure the audit will include a blower door test and thermal scanning.

A blower door test depressurizes the house using the same principle as turning on exhaust fans (described above in the do-it-yourself audit) but does so more effectively using a special fan and an air-pressure monitor that will determine the exact rate of air infiltration for the whole house.

While the blower door fan is running, the inspector will conduct a thermal scan using a special infrared camera. The images produced by this camera not only locate air leaks, but also show things not visible to the naked eye, such as where insulation is missing behind the walls. This is best done when there is a 20-degree difference between indoor and outdoor temperatures. Unlike the do-it-yourself test described above, which is best done in cold weather, an infrared scan works equally well on a warm day when the inside has been cooled by air-conditioning.

Most energy audits will also inspect heating and cooling equipment and ductwork, and identify other areas where energy can be saved. A duct blaster test, included in some audits or offered as an option, locates leaks in air ducts that can be responsible for a significant loss of efficiency.

After the audit you will receive a written report with images from the thermal scan and a detailed list of what can be done to make the house more comfortable and energy efficient.

◄ An energy auditor uses a hand-held infrared camera to locate differences in the temperature of a house's parts; images like these can indicate underinsulated areas, air leaks, and even moisture problems.

▼ The blue areas in this image show where insulation is missing.

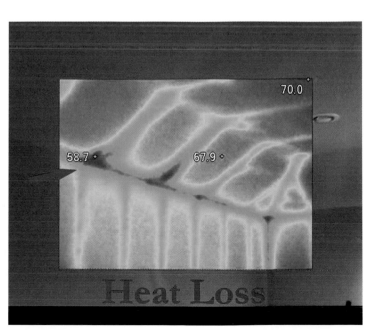

CREDITS

Chapter 5

p. 101: Photo © Hulya Kolabas
p. 102: Photos © Eric Roth, Architect: Tref LaFleche, LDa Architecture & Interiors
pp. 104–105: Photos © Jack Thompson, Contractor: Julie Groth, Step by Step Construction
p. 106: Photo courtesy Bill Boehm, Architect: Bill Boehm, Boehm Architecture
p. 107: Photo by David Yates, courtesy *Fine Homebuilding* magazine, © The Taunton Press, Inc.
p. 108: Photo © Art Grice, Architect: Jim Burton, BLIP DESIGN
p. 109: Photo courtesy Eric Doub, Ecofutures, Inc., ecofutures-building.com
p. 112: Photo © John Milo Beranek, Architect: Michael Klement, Architectural Resource
p. 114: Photo courtesy freewatt™ Micro-CHP Home Heating and Power System
p. 117: Photos © Hulya Kolabas, Architect: Hannah Purdy, Green Street Construction
p. 118: (left) Photo courtesy www.airgenerate.com; (right) Photo courtesy www.rightway-plumbing.org
p. 120: Photo courtesy Michael Klement
pp. 121–128: Photos © John Milo Beranek, Architect: Michael Klement, Architectural Resource

Chapter 6

p. 129: Photo © Lucas Fladzinski, Architect: William S. Duff, Jr., William Duff Architects
p. 130: Photo © iStockPhoto.com/Amanda Rohde
p. 131: Photo © Gilbertson Photography, Architect: Kevin Flynn, EcoDeep
p. 132: Photo courtesy ALSONS Corp.
p. 133: Photo © iStockPhoto.com/Odelia Cohen
p. 134: Photo © Gilbertson Photography, Architect: Kevin Flynn, EcoDeep
p. 135: Photo © Barry Katz, Logo courtesy US EPA/Watersense
p. 137: Photo courtesy ACT, Inc. Metlund Systems
p. 138: Photo M. Chandley, courtesy of Vanguard
p. 139: Photo © Hulya Kolabas, Architect: Hannah Purdy, Green Street Construction
p. 140: Photo courtesy US EPA, Energy Star Program
p. 141: (left) Photo © iStockPhoto.com/Sarah Musselman; (right) Photo © iStockPhoto.com/Terrance Emerson
p. 142: (top) Photo © Gilbertson Photography, Architect: Kevin Flynn, EcoDeep; (bottom) Photo © Greg Hursley, Architect: Al York, McKinney-York Architects

p. 146: (top) Photo courtesy Air & Water, Inc.; (bottom) Photo courtesy WattStopper
p. 147: (left) Photo courtesy P3 International; (middle) Photo courtesy Current Cost; (right) Photo courtesy The Energy Detective
pp. 149–151: Photos: Ken Wyner, Architect: Alan Abrams, Abrams Design Build
pp. 152–157: Photos © Ken Gutmaker, Architect: David Arkin, Arkin Tilt Architects

Chapter 7

p. 159: Photo © Eric Roth, Architect: Don Duffy, Don Duffy Architecture
p. 160 Photo courtesy Thompson Naylor Architects, Architect: Dennis Thompson, Thompson Naylor Architects
p. 161: (top) Photo © Eric Roth, Architect: Jeremiah Eck, Eck MacNeely Architects; (bottom) Photo © 1996 Forest Stewardship Council A.C.
p. 162: Photo: Eric Roth Architect: Ann M. Walters, Dewing & Schmid Architects
p. 164: (left) Photo © Barry Katz; (right) Photo courtesy Michael Klement
p. 165: (top) Photo courtesy Bill Boehm, Architect: Bill Boehm, Boehm Architecture; (bottom) Photo courtesy New Mexico Bureau of Geology and Mineral Resources
p. 166: (top) Photo by Dan Thornton, courtesy *Fine Homebuilding* magazine, © The Taunton Press, Inc.; (bottom) Photos courtesy Michael Klement
p. 168: Photo courtesy Bill Boehm
p. 169: (top) Photo courtesy Mountain Lumber; (bottom) Photos © John Milo Beranek, Architect: Michael Klement, Architectural Resource
p. 170: (top) Photo © Art Grice; (bottom) Photo courtesy Triton Logging
p. 171: (top left) Photo © Jack Thompson; (top right) Photo courtesy Squak Mountain Stone; (bottom left) Photo © Ken Gutmaker; (bottom right) Photo © Hulya Kolabas
p. 172: Photos © David Bergman, Architect: David Bergman Architect
p. 173: (left) Photo courtesy Cali Bamboo; (middle) Photo courtesy CorkFloor.com; (right) Photo courtesy Kirei USA
pp. 174–175: Photos © Bradley Khouri, Architect: Bradley Khouri, B9 Architects
p. 177: Photo © Eric Roth, Architect: Don Duffy, Don Duffy Architecture
p. 179: (top left) Photo courtesy Don Duffy; (top right & bottom) Photos © Eric Roth, Architect: Don Duffy, Don Duffy Architecture
pp. 180–181: Photos © Eric Roth, Architect: Don Duffy, Don Duffy Architecture

Chapter 8

p. 183: Photo © Trudy Dujardin
p. 184: Photo © Barry Katz
p. 185: Photo © Jonathan Leys/www.mrwoodmaster.com
p. 187: Photo © iStockPhoto.com/fotogeek4
p. 189: (left) Photo © Eric Roth Architect: Ann M. Walters, Dewing & Schmid Architects; (right) Photo © Gilbertson Photography, Architect: Kevin Flynn, EcoDeep
p. 190: Photo © Eric Roth, Architect: Tref LaFleche, LDa Architecture & Interiors
p. 191: (left) Photo by Karen Tanaka, courtesy *Inspired House* magazine, © The Taunton Press, Inc., Architect: Peabody Architects; (right) Photo © Barry Katz
p. 192: Photo by Chris Green, courtesy *Fine Homebuilding* magazine, © The Taunton Press, Inc., Designer: Al Rossetto
p. 193: (left) Photo © Jonathan Leys/www.mrwoodmaster.com; (right) Photo © Trudy Dujardin
p. 194: (top) Photo © Greg Auseth, Architect: Bryan Anderson, SALA Architects; (bottom) Photo © Greg Crawford, Architect: Svigals & Partners, Contractor: Barry Katz Homebuilding
p. 196: Photo by Karen Tanaka, courtesy *Inspired House* magazine, © The Taunton Press, Inc., Architect: Peabody Architects
p. 198: Photo courtesy www.greenecowalls.com
p. 200: Photo courtesy Bryan Anderson, SALA Architects
p. 201: Photo © Greg Auseth, Architect: Bryan Anderson, SALA Architects
pp. 203–205: Photos © Greg Auseth, Architect: Bryan Anderson, SALA Architects

Chapter 9

p. 207: Photo © Lucas Fladzinski, Architect: William S. Duff, Jr., William Duff Architects
p. 208: Photo © Trudy Dujardin
pp. 209–210: Photos © Hulya Kolabas, Architect: Hannah Purdy, Green Street Construction
p. 211: Photo © Trudy Dujardin, Designer: Trudy Dujardin, Dujardin Design Associates
pp. 212–213: Photos courtesy Wikimedia Commons
p. 214: Photo © Lucas Fladzinski, Architect: William S. Duff, Jr., William Duff Architects
p. 216: Photos courtesy Green Building Advisor, Architect: Chael, Cooper & Associates
p. 217: Photos © Matthew Ulrich, Designer: Matthew Ulrich & Assoc., Landscape Design
p. 218: Photo courtesy Hannah Purdy
pp. 219–225: Photos: © Hulya Kolabas, Architect: Hannah Purdy, Green Street Construction

p. 230: Photo by Chris Ermides, courtesy *Fine Homebuilding* magazine, © The Taunton Press, Inc.
p. 231: (left) Photo by Chris Ermides, courtesy *Fine Homebuilding* magazine, © The Taunton Press, Inc.; (right) Photo courtesy www.shininghomes.com

INDEX